WHAT TO DO...
WHEN YOUR CHILD HAS TROUBLE AT SCHOOL

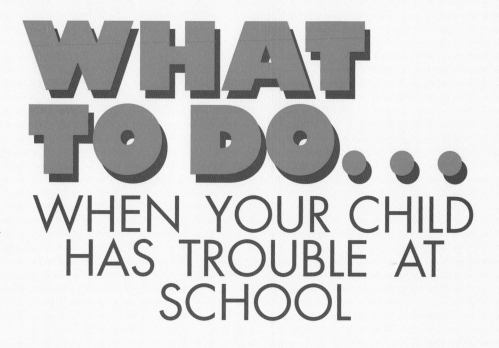

WHAT TO DO....
WHEN YOUR CHILD HAS TROUBLE AT SCHOOL

KAREN LEVINE

Reader's Digest

The Reader's Digest Association, Inc.
Pleasantville, N.Y./Montreal

Acknowledgments

I'd like to thank the many parents, students, and teachers who spoke so openly to me about their difficulties, in the hope that their candid accounts might make problems at school less painful for others. In all cases, their names have been changed to protect their privacy.

I'd also like to thank the many psychologists, psychiatrists, learning experts, and school administrators who made themselves and their research available to me, especially Judy David, David Anderegg, Edward Hallowell, Suzanne King, Susan Engel, Ursula Ferro, Lorenzo Licopoli, and Wendy Rubin.

I am indebted to my friend C. L. Fornari—who became a learning expert when it became clear that her children needed her to be one—for all of her sage counsel and fine referrals. I am grateful, as always, to my sons Noah and Nathaniel, who are extraordinarily generous in their willingness to let me share their lives with others; and to my husband, Alan, for his willingness to share a life with me . . . even when the bowl has more pits than cherries.

A Reader's Digest Book

Conceived, written, and produced by Pen & Pencil Books.
Reader's Digest Parenting Guide Series creators:
Elin McCoy (editorial); Judy Speicher (design)
Copyright © 1997 by Pen & Pencil Books LLC
All rights reserved. Unauthorized reproduction, in any manner, is prohibited.

Cover photograph: Mary Kate Denny/Tony Stone Images
Photographs: 7 Arthur Tilley/FPG International, 13 John Fortunato/Tony Stone Images, 19 Ron Rovtar/FPG International, 23 Ian Shaw/Tony Stone Images, 25 Ian Shaw/Tony Stone Images, 31 David Young-Wolff/Tony Stone Images, 33 Andy Sacks/Tony Stone Images, 37 Telegraph Colour Library/FPG International, 39 Ariel Skelley/The Stock Market , 41 Bruce Ayres/Tony Stone Images, 44 Jonathan Meyers/FPG International, 46 Mary Kate Denny/Tony Stone Images, 55 Arthur Tilley/FPG International, 61 Tom & Dee Ann McCarthy/The Stock Market , 65 Robert E. Daemmrich/Tony Stone Images, 66 David Young-Wolff/PhotoEdit, 70 Chip Henderson/Tony Stone Images, 77 David Young-Wolff/PhotoEdit, 80 Chad Slattery/Tony Stone Images, 83 David Hanover/Tony Stone Images, 87 Mary Kate Denny/Tony Stone Images, 91 Dan Bosler/Tony Stone Images.

Library of Congress Cataloging in Publication Data
Levine, Karen.
    What to do . . . when your child has trouble at school / Karen Levine.
        p.   cm. — (Reader's digest parenting guides)
    ISBN 0-89577-985-4
    1. Problem children—Education (Elementary)—United States.   2. Learning disabled children—Education (Elementary)—United States.   3. Education, Elementary—Parent participation—United States.   I. Title.   II. Series.
LC4802.L48   1997
371.93—dc21   97-2469

Reader's Digest and the Pegasus logo are registered trademarks of
The Reader's Digest Association, Inc.

Printed in the United States of America.

CONTENTS

Between the ages of five and thirteen, school is one of the main threads in the fabric of our children's lives. The day they start school is a big day for them—it's a step away from us into a world of teachers, other kids, and new skills and ideas. And it's just as big a day for parents, because it marks the beginning of a serious collaboration between us and our kids that continues throughout elementary and middle school. Since we want our kids to be happy and successful in school, we worry when they encounter the inevitable rough spots along the way.

Many of us don't know what to do when our kids run into trouble—or how to prevent it from happening—and we ask ourselves questions like these:

Why is Molly having such a hard time learning to read? How can I get Charlie to do his homework without a battle? Why does Alex have so much trouble with his teacher? The school counselor thinks we should have Amanda tested, but what does that mean? What home routines would help Tom do better at school?

It's one thing to have experts tell you that all kids experience school problems at some point or another, and it's quite another to really believe it. . . to not feel guilty. . . and to figure out what you can do to help.

That's what this book is about.

The first section, **Real Stories & Situations,** is filled with stories of real kids ages five to thirteen and the kinds of problems they've had at school. In **Understanding The Problem,** you'll find answers to basic questions parents have, from why children get into trouble at school to what effect a bad year has on them. **What To Do** offers practical solutions—actions that will help you and your kids cope with the typical problems of children in elementary and middle school and ways to prevent them. The fourth section, **Year By Year,** is a quick reference to what schools expect of kids at different ages and age-related signs of learning disabilities. **We Recommend** lists the best books and Internet sources on the subject to share with your children and to further your own understanding.

REAL STORIES & SITUATIONS

Is One Of These Your Child's Story?

SARAH, AGE 5, KINDERGARTEN

Sarah and her mom, Irene, had fun shopping for the clothes that Sarah needed for kindergarten. But the night before school started, when Irene laid out the new purple jumper and tights, Sarah announced, "I might not go."

"Hah, hah," Irene laughed, "That's a good joke."

But Sarah didn't smile.

The next day, when they got to the classroom, Sarah happily explored the costume corner and the cozy area for books, but when it was time for the good-bye kiss, she locked her arms around her mom's neck and wouldn't let go.

"Look at all the other girls and boys," Irene suggested, as she watched them calmly bidding their parents farewell. But Sarah, her face buried in Irene's neck, clung harder and wouldn't look up.

The teacher did her best to put Sarah at ease, showing her the huge crayon collection she had amassed over the years with every possible color under the rainbow, but Sarah still wouldn't let go of her mom. So Irene wound up spending the first week sitting right next to Sarah in the classroom and the following week sitting in the hall outside the classroom, just in case Sarah needed her.

She wondered, "Why is Sarah having such a hard time letting me leave? When will she be ready?"

JOSH, AGE 6, FIRST GRADE

Midway through the year, when Alan and Jean McCarthy were called in for a special conference by their son's first-grade teacher, they didn't know what to expect. Josh seemed to like school, but they hadn't heard much enthusiasm coming from Mrs. Granger, Josh's teacher.

"The good news," she said, as she looked through her folder of notes, "is that Josh is very bright and very social."

"And the bad news?" asked Alan McCarthy, in his usual forthright way.

"Well, I don't like the word 'bad,'" replied Mrs. Granger. "But Josh is a constant source of distraction in the classroom. He seems to need to be the center of attention. His hand is always up, and frequently he calls answers out of turn."

"That's because he knows so much," protested Jean McCarthy, a bit defensively.

"I realize that," said Mrs. Granger, "and his enthusiasm can be infectious. But there are times when there's a need to be quiet, and Josh doesn't always respect that. I don't want his behavior to get out of hand, so I thought I'd enlist your help in figuring out a solution."

But despite Mrs. Granger's goodwill and reassurances, the McCarthys left the conference feeling awful.

"We never had any of these problems with Eric," said Alan, referring to their studious older son.

ANNA, AGE 7, SECOND GRADE

Ever since she was in diapers, Anna's parents had read to her: *Goodnight Moon*, *Where the Wild Things Are*, *Bedtime for Frances*. The Lyonses were a family of great readers. But by second grade, Anna was still not a reader, and her parents simply couldn't understand it.

"All through first grade, Anna's teacher told us to relax and not to worry," Mrs. Lyons informed Anna's second-grade teacher, Mr. Washington.

"And we understood that pressure to read can backfire," added Mr. Lyons. "But now it's second grade, and Anna still seems to have trouble decoding simple words."

"It's true. But to be honest with you, I don't think Anna's problem is just with reading," said Mr. Washington. "Anna is always drifting off, as though she's on a balloon trip over the ocean. She really seems to have a hard time paying attention and staying on task."

"Is that so bad, to be a little dreamy?" Mr. Lyons asked. "I mean, she is just a kid."

"I know," said Mr. Washington. "And believe me, given the rowdy boys in this class, a little quiet and dreaminess doesn't always seem so bad. But sometimes I just lose sight of Anna. I have to remind myself not to forget about her."

"What can we do, Mr. Washington?" Anna's mother asked. "Is there something wrong with our daughter?"

JENNY, AGE 8, THIRD GRADE

This year Jenny has serious homework for the first time, and she doesn't like it. What really upsets her mom, Joanne, are the stormy battles they fight every day about when it should be done and how much time Jenny should spend working on it.

Jenny doesn't want to do her homework right after school, and her mom sympathizes with that. After all, Jenny is wound up from being cooped up all day at school and on the bus ride home. No wonder she wants to walk her balance beam in the backyard, go for a run with her puppy, and do all sorts of other things she likes to do, such as make "s'mores" out of chocolate, marshmallows, and graham crackers, and leave a mess in the microwave for her mom to clean up.

But after dinner seems no better. When Joanne says, "Time to start on your work," Jenny whines, "I'm too tired. I don't want to."

Eventually Joanne gets angry and Jenny's dad steps in. "I'll handle this," he says. "You're too easy on her. Get down to it, young lady," he warns. "What's happened to you? Last year we could have wallpapered the bathroom with the Happy Stickers on your homework papers."

"I'm doing it, aren't I?" Jenny says, as she puts her math book on the kitchen table. But a few minutes later, looking through her backpack, she says, "Uh-oh. I forgot my journal."

"That's the third time this week!" Jenny's dad explodes. "Well, I'm not driving over to the school to get it. Maybe if I don't, you'll learn your lesson."

GABE, AGE 9, FOURTH GRADE

The family joke in the Masarek household was that Gabe was "the absent-minded professor." He was a whiz at math, a killer chess player, and a computer game demon. But he was also terribly disorganized and very messy. "That kid couldn't find his way out of a paper bag," his brother Aaron rudely teased.

The problem was just as bad at school. On Gabe's report card, Mr. Laxer, the fourth-grade teacher, had written, "Gabe has a fine mind, but he rarely writes down his assignments and forgets to do the work, is always looking for a pencil or a book, and I can't even remember how many times I've had to lend him lunch money this term. His disorganization is interfering with his work in a serious way."

His parents tried everything. They bought him an assignment book, but he lost it. Now they even write him notes, but he forgets to look at them. His mom says, "We'd tie a string around Gabe's finger, but he'd probably lose his finger!"

Mr. Laxer came up with one homework solution that worked for a while: he sent a slip home with Gabe every day to be signed by Gabe's parents. But Gabe found it mortifying and, besides, it was just a Band-Aid on the bigger problem—the chaos inside Gabe's head.

The last straw was when his class went on a field trip, and Gabe had to spend the day in the school office because he didn't bring his permission slip—despite many reminders from his parents and Mr. Laxer.

SAM, AGE 10, FIFTH GRADE

Sam was Mr. Happy-Go-Lucky until he started fifth grade in the middle school.

"School has never been Sam's favorite place to be. You know that," Sam's mom, Sheila, confides to Jill, the mother of Sam's best friend, Jud, as they share a cup of coffee while waiting for the end of the boys' hockey practice.

"Yeah, but I bet he never puts up a stink about it the way Jud does," Jill says.

"Are you kidding? Sam's 'off' day is every day," Sheila retorts. "Every morning he has a stomachache or says he's coming down with a cold or his ankle feels as though he might have sprained it. I'm worried something is wrong at school."

"Have you spoken with his homeroom teacher about it?" Jill asks.

"Yes," Sheila says. "According to her, Sam is doing fine in school—he seems to have lots of friends, and the work comes easily to him. Jim and I have tried asking him what's wrong, but we get nowhere. We even floated the idea of looking at a private school."

"What does Sam say?" Jill asked.

"He claims he likes his school." Sheila looked pensive as she drained her coffee cup. "He says this year he just needs some time off every now and then."

MARISA, AGE 11, SIXTH GRADE

Jane Streeter finally made an appointment with the school psychologist to talk about her daughter, Marisa. She wasn't sure if she really needed to be so concerned about Marisa's up and down moods, but she was sure they were related to school.

"It doesn't have to be that 'important,'" said Dr. Rosen, a kind-faced woman in her late fifties. "Let's just talk."

"Well, some days, Marisa comes home happy as a clam, talking about glee club or her clay project in art. Other days when I ask how school was, I hear that whoever was her best friend the day before has now become her worst enemy. The teacher she loved is now the cruelest person in the world! And, on days like that, she can barely do her homework!" Jane exclaimed.

A few days later, an animated and chatty Marisa sat in the seat where her mother had sat. But when Dr. Rosen asked about her friends, a troubled look came over Marisa's face. "It's hard," she said in a voice that dropped to a whisper, "because you never know where you stand."

"What do you mean?" Dr. Rosen asked in her kind, calm way.

Marisa shrugged nervously. "Someone is always out, and when it's you, everyone dumps on you and you don't even feel like being in class."

"That must feel awful," said Dr. Rosen, commiserating with her.

"It does," Marisa murmured. "And how can you pay attention to your teacher, who's talking about the tides or Abraham Lincoln or something like that, when what you're really thinking about is who you're going to sit with at lunch or talk to in the hall when the bell rings?"

▶ PARENT TIPS

Check Your Own Reaction

▶ Sarah's mom, Irene, was embarrassed by Sarah clinging to her when all the other kids seemed to have an easier time letting their parents go. "Finally I realized making comparisons between her and the other kids probably made her feel worse. I had to forget my embarrassment and concentrate on how scared Sarah felt to know what to do to help her," she says.

▶ Josh's dad says, "My first thought was that I must have done something very wrong to have a kid who was causing this much trouble in first grade! But it dawned on me that I needed to look at the situation more objectively to help my son."

▶ Jenny's parents, frustrated by her lack of homework responsibility, were angry at her and blamed each other. "Neither of us could stand to see Jenny fail," her mom says. "By taking the responsibility for her homework and getting angry, we just kept the battles going. We had to stay calm and let Jenny know we were going to stick together on the rules."

JAMIE, AGE 12, SEVENTH GRADE

"If I hear the words 'school is boring' one more time," exclaimed Mr. Maxwell, "I'm going to explode! From now on, those words are outlawed in this house!"

Jamie looked at her mother, who was feeling sympathetic to her daughter because she had certainly never brought home such a report card before.

"Two Cs, a D, and a B! There's no excuse for a report card like this," Mr. Maxwell said angrily. "Next week when we meet with your teachers, I want you there."

"I can't help it," Jamie wailed. "School is so bor. . .uninteresting all the time," she quickly amended.

"Do you think maybe you're being a little hard on her?" Jamie's mom asked after Jamie left the room.

"Absolutely not," Jamie's dad replied. "That kid has an IQ of 130. She can do much better."

At the conference, when Jamie used the "B" word to describe why she wasn't motivated, Mr. Maxwell appealed to Jamie's teachers. "So what's the problem, folks? What can we do to help my daughter?"

It turned out that Jamie was bored because the work just wasn't demanding enough for her. Many of the girls with whom she had been friendly in the past, and who had been good students, were now also slipping academically.

EZRA, AGE 13, EIGHTH GRADE

As they went through the basement, clearing out old junk for a new generation of junk, Carl and Lissa Fanzoni came across a box of Legos that their son Ezra had so loved when he was six.

"Do you remember the way he'd play with these for hours?" Lissa recalled. "And then it was models—he used to have such an attention span for things like that. What do you think happened?"

Carl shrugged. "I don't know. If someone had told me that my hard-working six-year-old would grow up to be my lazy thirteen-year-old, whose idea of getting schoolwork done is to do it in the fastest, sloppiest, least involved way possible, I wouldn't have believed it."

"Maybe it's just the way kids are today," Lissa suggested.

"I don't know," Carl said, shaking his head again. "Did you see that history homework he handed in a few days ago? Talk about short answer questions. If something can be said in three words, he'll try to say it in two."

"I wouldn't care," Lissa said wistfully, "if I felt he was passionate about something at school—even basketball or swimming or some other after-school activity! Anything! Just so long as he could get the feeling of working hard at something and getting better as a result of his work." ❏

UNDERSTANDING THE PROBLEM

Answers To Basic Questions

Why Do Kids Have Trouble At School?

We don't like to think of our child's school career as a minefield of potential problems awaiting one wrong step. It's much more pleasant to think about school as a garden where our kids will grow and blossom—intellectually, academically, and emotionally.

But as most parents quickly learn, school is both. The very aspects of school that offer our children a chance to grow can also present hazards. It helps to remind ourselves that very few kids make it through the years of elementary and middle school without running into at least one of those hazards.

One year your child may draw a terrible teacher, the next be lost in long division, and the next feel that he or she hasn't a single friend in the class. Though some problems are more exhausting and challenging than others, they're usually manageable. If we understand where trouble at school is likely to develop, we can help our kids succeed instead of scrape by. I've found that kids may encounter trouble in four areas.

Troubles with teachers

Did you ever think about how important and powerful teachers are in your child's life? Kids spend more time each day with teachers than they do with any other adult except their parents, and possibly a grandparent or other relative or caregiver. Before school the only adult personalities that our kids have to adapt to are us and maybe a babysitter. Now teachers join those ranks, and as we all know, they vary widely in style and personality. They can make children feel proud or ashamed of themselves, smart or dumb, pleasant to be with or a pain. No wonder so many problems can arise between kids and teachers!

Guess which teacher a child with a great sense of humor will better adapt to—one who loves to laugh or one who is humorless? Some teachers are no-nonsense, businesslike, and tolerate very little deviation from their way of doing things, while others are warm, flexible, and nurturing, and still

---

▶ **PARENT TIPS**

If your child clashes with the school's culture:

▶ "Talk with the teacher about your family," advises Lee's dad. Lee's teacher complained that Lee monopolized the conversation during circle time. But at the conference she learned it wasn't out of disrespect for others; rather, Lee was an only child used to expressing himself with enthusiasm and passion at home and needed help learning to understand group priorities.

▶ "Talk with your child about differences," advises Karen's mom. Karen's teacher said she was too competitive in her cooperative math group. "We talked to Karen about the ways in which our family is highly competitive," Karen's mom explained, "and how being cooperative is important, too."

▶ "Approach differences in a positive way," say both families. "We spent a lot of time talking about what a boring world it would be if everyone were the same," Lee's dad said. "And we talked about how the families around us differed from one another."

others are downright mean and sarcastic and don't seem to like kids very much. Some are very much like mom or dad, while others seem to play by an entirely different set of rules—and to succeed in the world of school our children have to learn how to "read" those rules. Kids who can will understand quickly, for example, that Mrs. Kahn sounds gruff when you forget your homework, but that if you apologize, she'll forget about it.

Some children find the task of adjusting to a particular teacher extremely difficult. They may talk back or rebel, or, as was the case with Judy, a second grader, they may be completely intimidated. At the end of Judy's first day in second grade, she came home one afternoon with wet pants, terribly upset. She had raised her hand to ask to go to the bathroom, but the teacher didn't call on her, and she was afraid to get up and ask for a bathroom pass. Her teacher wasn't an ogre, but she did have a very stern manner. Another child, though, probably wouldn't have been so scared.

Troubles with schoolwork

Many parents tend to think of the academic part of school as the most important piece, and forget that schoolwork is not just a matter of whether you understand how to add and subtract fractions or find reading easy or hard. Most kids do have at least occasional difficulty with a specific subject, like reading or science, but often their problems are more general.

During elementary and middle school our children gradually learn the skills that underlie all learning—how to study, how to organize themselves and their papers, how to follow through on assignments and plan ahead, how to be motivated and focus their attention, and how to recognize when they don't understand something like long division and get the help they need. Of course, to our despair, they rarely learn these skills in a systematic way—and that's one reason troubles start.

Sorting out what a schoolwork problem is about is not always easy because it can be simple or complex, general or specific, serious or superficial—and the solutions can be the same. A conference with a fifth-grade teacher over Sandy's failure to hand in assignments was solved quickly with study/assignment sheets for her parents to sign. But sometimes, testing by an expert is necessary to figure it all out.

Problems with other kids

One of the biggest adjustments children have when they start school is moving from the one-on-one environment of home to the group environment of the classroom. As we all know, getting along with others in a group isn't always easy, especially when you're thrown together with the same individuals day after day whether you like them or not! It's hard to learn you can't always be the center of attention, that others may be better than you are at writing or baseball, that not every child in a class of twenty or more will be your friend.

Though a few kids—usually someone else's—always seem to get along with everyone, most have a bumpy time. They act out by hitting someone on the playground, teasing and calling names when the teacher isn't looking, or sitting shyly in a corner, convinced that this year no one likes them. Let's face it: part of school, especially in these years from kindergarten through eighth grade, is learning to find a comfortable place among your peers.

Your child's personality may cause problems, and schools vary in their ability to handle them. Those that emphasize group work give the teacher an opportunity to observe and help kids learn to get along, but the same setting may be very distracting for children like my younger son, whose social antennae take in everything within a ten-mile radius.

How your child relates to other kids can also have a profound impact on his schoolwork, particularly during those middle-school years when social issues are paramount. A sixth grader who is always the last one picked for the soccer team during gym, for example, may be too distracted by a dread of gym class to pay attention in the class right before it.

Problems with the culture of the school

Though we don't often think about it, each school has its own culture, which has both written and unwritten rules. Sometimes our kids clash with that culture, as Toni did, and problems result. In her house, conversation is noisy and animated, and her parents encourage and are intrigued by the questions she asks, particularly when she challenges the status quo. Toni's school, on the other hand, has a fairly rigid structure—authority is not to be challenged, and children are expected to raise their hands to ask questions and speak quietly. Until Toni could adapt to and abide by the school culture, she kept getting into trouble.

This issue of the school's culture can be quite subtle. Think about the kind of family you have. Do you value order or do you find disorder stimulating? Do you value differences or do you find comfort in conformity? Do you run a loose, open kind of home ("How many for dinner tonight?") or are you more relaxed with predictability? Is everyone in your family highly competitive or do you encourage cooperation?

Children do mature when they learn to adapt to and work in different environments—after all, that's part of what kids learn once they go outside their own homes to school! But sometimes adjusting is hard, and when it is, parents may need to help their kids learn how. ❏

Does A School's Atmosphere Contribute To Kids' Problems?

When you walk into a school—or a classroom—you can tell a lot just by looking around. Does it have a lively, messy look or is it very neat and orderly? Do you hear a buzz of children's voices or is it hushed and quiet? Is there something about the way children walk down the hall that suggests camaraderie or do most kids seem to be on their own?

There is no single kind of school that is perfect for all kids. Different kinds of kids feel safe and happy in different kinds of environments. The trouble is that unless your child is in one where he feels safe and happy and that fits with his style of learning, he'll have problems. My younger son, for example, spent kindergarten and first grade in a school where all kinds of interesting activities were going on, and the walls, cluttered with fascinating kid-made art and writing, reflected this. I was very comfortable there but it turned out not to be a good fit for my son, who was so distracted by everything going on that he accomplished very little. In second grade, at the local public school, the walls were less crowded and so was his plate—and he started to focus.

Defining atmosphere

All sorts of factors make up a school's atmosphere. For starters, there's the school's philosophy. Some schools foster competition, others emphasize cooperative learning, and still others combine the two. If your child is naturally competitive, he won't feel good about himself in a school that regards competition as a character flaw—and he's likely to end up in trouble.

The rules that guide school behavior also matter. Most children, but all shy, timid ones, do better in schools with clear limits regarding bullying and strong guidelines about how to treat fellow students with respect. On the other hand, a highly social child will probably do fine even if the school's emphasis is on learning to ignore hurtful behavior and standing up for yourself when the going gets tough.

Classroom atmosphere counts, too. Easily distracted kids, like my son, may

---

▶ PARENT TIPS

Parents suggest asking these questions to check out the atmosphere at your child's school:

- ► How does the principal treat teachers and parents?
- ► How do the teachers talk about the principal?
- ► How does your child's teacher talk to the children and respond to their ideas?
- ► How are conflicts between children resolved?
- ► Do teachers encourage and help kids to problem solve?
- ► Is the playground viewed as a part of the school environment? Is behavior there monitored?
- ► Do kids help generate the rules of the classroom?

• **Vivian Gussin Paley, a MacArthur Foundation Fellow who teaches kindergarten at the University of Chicago Laboratory Schools, believes that for young children being safe also means not worrying about rejection.**

  She conducted an experiment in which children were not permitted to say, "You can't play" to their classmates. Every time the rule was broken the children analyzed the rule along with the behavior. By the end of the year the entire class had a genuine awareness and sensitivity to the feelings of their classmates.

have no problems in a structured environment, while others rebel and work better in an open classroom with more individual choices and projects. A child who tries hard but has difficulty with some subjects may be more successful in a school where teachers praise children for their effort rather than focusing on what they produce.

An atmosphere of unfairness

But some school and classroom environments aren't conducive to learning and actually create problems. Take Sarah's third-grade class, where the atmosphere was unhappy because the teacher favored one particular girl, Suzy, and always chose her to do the special jobs. All the students were angry at Suzy, naturally, and they were all angry at the teacher.

By the end of the term most students in the class felt, "Why bother? The teacher's never going to like us as much as she likes Suzy, anyway." Sarah, who began the year by caring very much about pleasing her teacher, stopped trying to do her best work. Joey started talking back to the teacher and became a "problem kid." His real problem was his teacher's unfairness.

Children also have problems with learning when they don't feel safe, like Ned, who was bullied and teased in middle school for being different. A boy who liked to play "girl" games more than "boy" games, he preferred acting in plays to

sports, and figure skating to hockey. When his grades began to drop and he talked about hating school, his parents met with his teachers and the principal. "Middle-school kids are very tough on each other. There's not much we can do about it," the principal said. He didn't see that the school's unwillingness to insist on tolerance and respect actually allowed the bullying to exist. Finally, because Ned was doing so poorly, his parents enrolled him in a small, experimental public school in a neighboring district, and there he thrived.

Is life unfair? You bet it is. Should children experience this unfairness in school? Absolutely not!

The impact on self-esteem

Just as a bad school atmosphere can make learning more difficult, a good one can enhance both learning and self-esteem.

Experts say that one effective way to establish a classroom that fosters learning is to involve kids in making the rules. These can be simple—"No hitting" or "No name-calling"—but also spark much thought and discussion. First graders who make a rule that outlaws name-calling may discuss how it feels to be called names. Research has shown that when kids are really involved in establishing the classroom's social dynamics, they come away with a big boost in self-esteem and are more likely to follow the rules. ❏

Change of any sort is difficult for children and adults alike. For most of us, the days are anchored by routines—the same breakfast, the same faces, our feet tracing the same old routes. The danger is that this sameness can get boring. But often it's easier for our children—as well as some of us—to cope with boredom than it is to face the unknown.

We tend to forget that for our children, school is uncharted territory. Each year there's a new teacher, a new classroom, and some years even a new school with new kids. It helps to remember that some children take much longer than others to get used to new places, no matter what their age. A child's temperament, flexibility, and personality account for much of the difference.

But surprises always sabotage any big transition—whether into kindergarten, first grade, a new school, middle school, or high school. The best way to ease these transitions for your child is to make everything as familiar as you possibly can.

Entering kindergarten

By the time most of our kids start kindergarten they've already experienced some separation from us by being in daycare or

nursery school. That experience helps ease the first few days, but not entirely. Unlike preschool, kindergartens are usually part of a bigger school with bigger kids. To some children, that's very scary. Moreover, what kindergarten teachers expect from children with regard to independence, work, and making friends is very different from the expectations of daycare and nursery school (see pages 87-90 for specific expectations). Many children have a hard time adjusting to that change and often temporarily behave as they did when younger.

Jody, who had been in nursery school since she was two and had never had a problem getting along with other kids or sharing, walked into her kindergarten class the first day and, much to her mother's horror, immediately grabbed a book from another little girl's hand. Her classmate, Andrew, who'd spent three wonderful years in family daycare, clung to his mother desperately and refused to let go of her leg.

Change creates stress for kids, and that means they need extra support from us. Making a child feel bad about his or her fears when starting school usually creates pressure and makes matters worse. If your child needs you and you can arrange time off from work, rest assured that you won't be the first parent to spend a few days in a kindergarten classroom!

It's a transition for parents, too!

Our children aren't the only ones who have difficulty with beginning school. Don't be surprised if you feel like Ann's mother, who was shocked and surprised by her own reaction to her daughter's first day of kindergarten. "I couldn't believe how lost I felt," she admits. "I was supposed to feel great about opening up my car door and watching Ann march into school with the other kids, but the truth is that I drove off with tears in my eyes. I had a very hard time letting go." Sometimes we don't realize how easily our children pick up on these feelings, and as a result have an even harder time letting go of us.

▶ PARENT TIPS

Before children start a new school, parents suggest:

- ▶ Talk about how much fun you had in school and what a wonderful experience your child will have.
- ▶ Make playdates for your child with children who will be in the class.
- ▶ Visit the school and classroom together.
- ▶ Meet the principal and the teacher.
- ▶ Find out as much as possible about the expectations of the program in which your child will be enrolled.
- ▶ Write down questions with your child before your visit.
- ▶ Find a way to volunteer, so that people know who you are and your child knows that you're familiar with the school.
- ▶ Take care of health forms, immunizations, and other red tape so that your child doesn't spend the first day sitting in the main office.

First grade: big expectations

Though every new school year is a transition, some are more momentous than others. First grade is a "biggie" to kids as well as parents. It means the beginning of "real school" and growing up. That's exciting and scary and sad.

One of the most difficult things about transitions—for anyone—is letting go of what you've come to love. Kindergarten, as most of our first graders recall with nostalgia, was warm and fuzzy and all about play. First grade, on the other hand, is about sitting still, following directions, holding all your good ideas in because it's someone else's turn to talk, and then forgetting what you wanted to say when your turn finally arrives. First grade is about learning to read and write and add. First grade is about work!

After an initial period of excitement at being more grown up, some children go through a very difficult period, longing for what they remember as the easier life of kindergarten.

And sometimes, as many parents have observed, our children's expectations are unrealistic and doomed to disappointment—like T.J.'s. As he got off the school bus after his first day in first grade, he burst into tears. "I still can't read," he complained to his mother. "The teacher didn't give us reading books or even say anything about reading! I'm not going back."

All summer long T.J. had been anticipating first grade as the time when he would learn how to read. We can help our children by asking in advance what their expectations are and gently bringing them in line with reality.

Know your child

During the years before school we learn how our children react to change and can use that knowledge to help them—and ourselves—through school transitions. Mary Ellen, for example, wasn't worried when her daughter announced that she hated school two weeks after first grade began. She knew her daughter was usually wildly enthusiastic about any new experience, then became upset after reality set in. So she didn't worry, and just said, "Let's see how you feel next week."

Because I knew that my second son was uncomfortable in unfamiliar places and especially uncomfortable having anyone know that he was uncomfortable, I knew starting kindergarten wouldn't be easy unless he knew what to expect in advance.

So before school began, we spent an hour one afternoon helping his teacher organize supplies and decorate the room. By the time we left, it was all very familiar to my son, and he walked into the classroom on the first day feeling excited instead of scared. ❏

What Makes Middle School So Tough?

After a month of middle school it was clear to Matt's parents that things weren't going well for their former star student. One night he forgot his spelling words and became hysterical when his mom suggested he call a friend for them. "I'm not a dork!" he cried. Then, after dinner, he sat down to do his math homework and discovered that he'd left his workbook in his locker—along with his gym clothing, which he was supposed to bring home to be washed. Matt's mom drove to school to pick up the forgotten items. The next morning Matt called home from school, nearly in tears. "I left my gym shorts on the table," he whispered. "Please, please bring them to school." Matt's parents were worried. Why was he having such trouble?

A time of new challenges

Whether kids begin middle school in fifth grade, as Matt did, or start junior high in sixth or seventh grade, many find the transition difficult and confusing. When you stop to think about it, the reasons are pretty apparent. For one thing, instead of spending all day in a single classroom with the same twenty to thirty kids and occasionally being herded down to the music room by the teacher, kids are responsible for getting themselves from one classroom to the next according to a tight schedule and must adapt to an ever-shifting group of classmates. Since most middle schools today draw students from several different elementary schools, they don't know most of the kids when school starts and may end up, as Matt did, in classes in which they don't have a single old friend. And middle schools usually have many more students than elementary schools.

The teacher situation is more complicated than in lower grades, too. Instead of having one teacher whom students get to know very well—and who also knows them—they now confront as many as six or seven teachers every day, each with a different way of doing things and different expectations. Changes that seem simple to us may contribute to kids' disorganization.

Coping with other changes

Entering middle school is also tricky because it coincides with a time when children are beginning another transition, too—within their own bodies. The discrepancy in size and physical maturity among middle schoolers is enough to make one's jaw drop. As a rule, girls are much more developed than boys and significantly taller, but differences are apparent even among children of the same sex. Jan was as tall as her mother and fully developed by the time she started sixth grade. Her best friend, Ellen, barely reached her shoulder and didn't even need a training bra. Tommy had a mustache and enough body odor for everyone to notice by the end of fifth grade, while John looked almost exactly the same as he had in second. Coping with internal and external change in concert can be exhausting—both for our kids and for us!

New social pressures

One thing new middle schoolers do with their social and academic anxiety is find a peer to "dump on." If you think back to your own childhood, you may remember how intense social pressures are in fifth and sixth grades. Kids are just beginning to develop a sense of who they are socially, and peer pressure to perform athletically and academically, to not perform academically, to dress in a certain way, and to be "in" with the right group is very serious

and important to your child. No matter how silly this seems to you, it's important to listen with empathy and respect. Keep in mind that by the time they leave middle school, they'll have a much stronger sense of who they are and where they fit in.

Parents' interest in school still matters

Many parents compound their kids' difficulty in adjusting to middle school because, research has found, they simply stop being as involved with school as they were during their children's elementary school years. This is partly a response to their children's bids for independence. Twelve-year-old Julie, for example, told her parents she was "mortified" because they called her homeroom teacher about a problem she had mentioned. It's also because parents don't always realize how confused and disorganized their kids are. From ages eleven to thirteen, mumbled, monosyllabic responses about how school is going are the norm and requests for help are few and far between.

Checking in with children regularly to make sure their work and papers are organized lets them know you still have clear expectations about academic work and gives them a chance to take you up on what should still be every parent's ongoing offer: Do you need any help? But after you do give help, bow out and let them take over tasks themselves. ❏

ADVICE FROM KIDS

What's the best way to handle cliques?

○ "If someone is getting teased a lot, they should just not listen. Don't let them see that they get to you," says Isaac, 11.

○ "If you're on the outside looking in, don't let them know how hurt they make you feel. Those people aren't worth taking up space in your mind," advises Lara, 12.

○ "If you're in a clique, don't take part in all the mean stuff. Also, it helps to know that everyone takes a turn at being dumped on," reports Ariana, 11.

○ "Hang out with different people instead of just with one bunch," offers Marissa, 13.

Do Some Kinds Of Kids Have More School Troubles?

In a word, yes. Kids with a lot of problems at school usually have one thing in common: they stand out, in one way or another, as being different.

Sasha was different in an academic way—he needed more time than his classmates with writing assignments, and his third-grade teacher insisted everyone complete the work within a given amount of time. If you didn't, you had to finish it during recess. Sasha stayed in every day. By November he hated school and was getting into fights. And by the time Thanksgiving rolled around, his teacher called his parents to discuss his "stubborn" and "lazy" behavior.

Jenna was different socially. She loved to read more than almost anything else. During recess, she rarely joined the other girls in games; instead, she put her nose in a book. As a result, she had practically no friends, and her teacher was worried.

Why differences matter

It's not too hard to imagine how children who are much smarter or slower than their classmates can have both social and academic problems. But even a difference like asking many more questions than others do can get a child into hot water with a teacher and other kids, while kids who never ask anything at all may be totally ignored. Kids who are extremely tall or extremely short, very fat or stick thin may be teased constantly. Then there are those

children who simply seem to march to their own drum.

All of these children can become "problems" because their differences interfere with the smooth operation of a school or classroom. Schools, after all, are little societies, and unless you have a gifted teacher who can see the value of "differentness"—and make everyone else see it as well—they run most smoothly when everyone conforms. Kids who are average in everything may have the easiest time.

Of course, those very same kids who stand out as being different may also be the most talented, the most insightful, the most sensitive, and, eventually, the most successful adults. But unless a child learns to manage his differentness so it doesn't interfere with the smooth running of his school or goes to a school that values diversity, he's likely to have problems.

Be an interpreter

Most children need our help in figuring out how to manage their differences, especially when they're academic. The most effective way we can do this is to act as interpreters and help teachers understand our children.

Sasha's mom, for example, explained to the teacher that Sasha was a very slow writer because he had a hard time with handwriting. Could he perhaps complete his work at home or use the classroom computer? She also gently mentioned Sasha's need to run after he'd been sitting still for a while in order to concentrate on further work. It would actually be "helpful and productive," she suggested, if he did run around the playground a few times. Keeping him in robbed him of physical release and humiliated him in front of his peers. No wonder Sasha dealt with both of those problems by socking someone!

If we do a good job as interpreters we can prevent our kids from being labeled—"bully," "lazy," "troublemaker," and so on. That's much easier than changing labels once they've been made.

Convey a sense of respect

As you can imagine, "interpreting" requires sensitivity to teachers. You want them to understand that you are attempting to be helpful, rather than challenging their authority. Under some circumstances it's hard not to be annoyed with a particular teacher, but beginning with "I wonder if ...." "You've probably noticed ...." or "Is there any way ...." usually works much better than angry words and confrontation.

Kids who don't have problems

As a rule, children who are different but who don't have problems are able to do four things: They tune in and adapt to what their teachers want; know how to ask teachers for help; know how to

be flexible when necessary; and decide that being different is part of their identity.

When Aaron entered public school after attending a Jewish school for six years, for example, he told his parents that he planned to wear his yarmulke (skull cap) to school, even though they thought he might be teased. Because this "different" piece of his identity was important to Aaron, he was able to project a positive attitude about it to his classmates and never had a problem. ❑

How Does Home Life Affect Your Child's Life At School?

When children are in elementary and middle school, home and school are the two most important parts of their lives. What happens at one usually affects the other. On the home-to-school route, our children carry with them both family problems that worry them and family values about learning. Kids are barometers of their environment.

When things are good . . .

When children come from homes in which reading, thinking, problem solving, open discussion, and mutual respect are important, they invariably do better in school, as research has shown over and over again. What we do at home reflects our attitudes about education, and our kids pick up on them all. If we visit museums and attend concerts, our children grow up with the feeling that these things are important. If we spend an hour every night reading or playing chess or Scrabble, they learn that there are ways to entertain themselves that don't involve turning on the tube and just watching passively.

. . . And when there's a problem

We also know that kids who are dealing with problems on the home front—such as divorce, a new sibling, an ill or dying grandparent, or anything else that shakes their security—are more likely to have behavior and learning difficulties in school.

Sometimes we forget that our kids' worries about problems at home are frequently expressed in their behavior in the classroom instead of to us. When Amy's grandmother suffered a stroke and her mom flew down to Florida to be with her, Amy couldn't seem to concentrate on third-grade spelling or math—she was busy worrying about what her grandma would be like the next time she saw her and if her mom would always be crying from now on. If we don't encourage our children to talk about family problems at home, we can be sure they will bring them to school!

The subtle influence of home

Lately, I've found myself thinking about the subtle ways in which home life encourages school success. Before our children reach school age, we're very conscious of our role as "first teachers." Most of us remember the many times we turned a run-of-the-

▶ PARENT TIPS

When parents are getting divorced:

▶ "When my husband and I separated, Sari was in sixth grade. Her father and I made an appointment with her team of teachers to let them know what was happening. We could barely stand to be in a room together, but we wanted Sari to see that we both felt her education was important and that we'd both continue to be involved," explains Moira, mother of 2.

mill trip to the supermarket into an educational field trip for our toddlers.

Yet once our kids enter school, many of us abdicate this role. Of course, we do the obvious things—buying the school supplies they need, seeing to it that they get adequate sleep and food, setting aside quiet time every night for homework, and being available to help. All this clearly has a positive effect. But many school problems can be avoided if we maintain the attitude we had when our children were in strollers—that we are their guides in a world filled with interesting learning opportunities. That's what Will's parents did.

In first grade Will was fascinated by birds, so his mom helped him build a bird feeder and hang it outside the kitchen window. Every day Will spent time watching birds at the feeder, so his parents bought him a guide to local birds, and his dad showed him how to look up what he observed. A few weeks later he and his mom started a bird chart. Will drew pictures of birds he observed and recorded their names and the dates he saw them. Other members of the family helped. His dad, an early riser, checked to see which birds turned up then. The project enthralled the family for one winter.

Will was being a "scientist"—someone who makes observations and records them. But he also learned that his family would support his interests and enthusiasm, and

this, too, had a positive impact on Will's schoolwork and attitudes toward school.

When home and school clash

Unfortunately, there's usually at least one time when parents don't see eye-to-eye with their child's teacher. It's a delicate situation. When we talk with our children, it's easy to fall into blaming, labeling, or putting the teacher down in an effort to show kids we understand what they're going through. But this often backfires. Our children pick up on our lack of respect for the teacher and end up in trouble.

Cara's dad, for example, didn't like the books her sixth-grade teacher chose for reading. "What a moron that teacher is," he said offhandedly. "Why can't he come up with some worthwhile reading?" It's not so surprising that Cara developed a contemptuous attitude toward her teacher and came to believe, "Everything at school is stupid!"

A better approach when we think a classroom rule is foolish, disagree with the way a teacher is covering a subject, or object to the handling of a behavior problem, is to talk directly with the teacher.

We sometimes forget just how much our children copy us. If we are unhappy with their teacher or school, they are likely to be unhappy, too. And if we treat schoolwork in a casual, disinterested way, they pick up a message that we don't think it's very important. ❏

What Are The Most Common Learning Disabilities?

To parents and teachers, a child with learning disabilities often looks much like a child with many ordinary school problems, such as doing poorly on tests, being disorganized, not paying attention in class, having trouble memorizing math facts, and getting into fights. That's one of the confusing things about learning disabilities—frequently the problems are not what they appear to be. Plus, there are many different learning disabilities, including a number that are subtle, complex, and hard to detect.

Cynthia's experience with her son, Mark, was typical. It took several frustrating years before Mark was finally diagnosed with learning disabilities. "During that time," Cynthia recalls, "we were caught up in worrying about and trying to fix the individual symptoms—the daydreaming, the sloppiness, the lack of organization, the aggressive behavior. And on and on. But when the big picture was clear and we knew which learning disabilities Mark had, it all finally made sense. Until then, we felt frustrated and irritated and sometimes angry with our own child."

What is a learning disability?

If you're like most parents, as well as most teachers and kids, you're confused about what "learning disability" actually means. And now experts are also using other terms, such as "learning disorder," "learning challenge," and "learning difference." It's helpful to think of all these as umbrella terms that cover a very wide range of educational problems. They include problems children have with listening, speaking, writing, reading, interpreting, understanding, and remembering.

Though experts don't know what causes many of these problems, we do know they usually have something to do with how an individual's brain works; they're not caused by handicaps such as mental retardation, blindness, or deafness, or by

▶ PARENT TIPS

Parents who have been through it offer this advice:

▶ "Create a support network for yourself by talking to other parents of children with learning disabilities," suggests Mary, mother of 3.

▶ "Offering praise and criticizing behavior, rather than character, is especially important with kids who have disabilities. 'I want the laundry picked up from your floor' is better than 'You're such a slob!'" says Jon, father of 1.

▶ "Help your child be successful by making instructions as specific as possible and dividing large tasks into smaller ones," offers Tina, mother of 2.

▶ "Don't let your child go into a new situation without preparing him or her for what may crop up. Kids with learning disabilities often have a harder time thinking on their feet," advises Richard, father of 2.

▶ "Be supportive of your child's teacher—teachers, like parents, can be frustrated when kids have learning problems. Win over the teacher by making yourself available as much as possible," says Ginny, mother of 3.

poor instruction. Kids who have them have the same intellectual potential as other children; they just have to learn things in different ways. Some mild learning problems are the result of a developmental lag: a child is behind his peers but will easily catch up with a little help and as he grows older. Learning difference has come to mean that a child has an unusual style of learning, such as needing to see everything written down in order to remember it. Learning disability is sometimes reserved for more serious problems.

Experts are beginning to recognize that even children and adults who don't have learning problems may have distinct learning styles. Just think of the process you use to memorize something, attack a math problem, or organize information you've read, and compare it with how a friend or spouse does the same thing.

Kinds of learning disabilities

The easiest way to understand learning disabilities is to think of them in terms of categories. Children can have problems in the way they take information in with their eyes, ears, and other senses; in the way they sort and store information; and/or in the way they communicate information verbally or in writing.

The disabilities that follow are the most common. Keep in mind that each has a wide range, from mild to severe. One child may need special help to improve his poor handwriting; another may need an occupational therapist to help him learn how to hold a pencil. Some kids may have only one problem; some may have several.

Language learning problems

Generally, these are difficulties in learning how to use language—reading, writing, organizing a written report, and also expressing ideas in words, which Mark, Cynthia's son, had trouble with.

Dyslexia is a problem with decoding written words, as children must be able to do in order to read. Children with dyslexia see the words on the page but they don't make sense. To a dyslexic child the printed words might look upside down or backward, so he would read "was" as "saw." But if you read the page aloud to the same child, he would probably have no trouble understanding what you read.

Dysgraphia is a neurologically based problem with writing. A child may have a pattern in mind, like the formation of a letter—or actually be looking at a pattern and trying to copy it—but be unable to transfer it to paper. Children with mild dysgraphia often just have poor handwriting, but some kids have so much trouble they need to use a keyboard.

Auditory perceptual disorders refer to kids' inability to identify, organize, and interpret information that they hear.

ADVICE FROM KIDS

Survival techniques from kids with learning disabilities.

○ "Never say 'NO' when your folks suggest an after-school tutor. It can make everything much, much easier," suggests Jennie, 12.

○ "Get someone to help you break things down into small steps and make a list," says Simon, 10.

○ "Learn about how you learn, so you can figure out ways to study that are best for you," counsels Ryan, 13.

○ "Spend time doing the stuff you really love—like snowboarding. It feels great to be good at something," says Matt, 9.

Elaine, for example, couldn't distinguish many rhyming words. "Blue" and "glue" sounded like the same word to her, but when she saw them on the printed page, she knew which was which. Like many children who have these problems, Elaine had trouble following oral directions and didn't remember assignments the teacher announced in class.

Visual perceptual disorders refer to kids' inability to identify, organize, and interpret information they look at. A child with this kind of disability probably wouldn't be able to learn spelling words by looking at them, but could by hearing them.

Memory problems

Short-term memory problems. Think of the brain as a workbench. A child who has a short-term memory problem has a workbench that gets crowded very quickly. With no place to put the information, it's gone! Ellen, a fifth grader, read a chapter about the Civil War in her history textbook for a quiz the next day. She understood it, and at dinner had a long discussion with her parents about the implications of the Civil War and why it is still meaningful today. But the next day all she could remember was that it was between the North and South, and that Lincoln was the President.

Long-term memory problems. Children with long-term memory problems have enough room in their workbench for storage, but after a period of time they can't recall where it is they've stored things. These are kids who often feel that they have an answer on the tip of their tongues and, when they hear the right answer say, quite honestly, "Oh yeah! I knew that!"

Organizational problems

Information processing disorder is an inability to organize, interpret, and store information after it has been received through the senses. Reel off a list of instructions to a child with a processing disorder and, at worst, she'll become paralyzed; at best, she'll become confused. Saying, "Take a bath, brush your teeth, and get into your pajamas," may result in a child putting on her pajamas (because it's the last thing she heard) and then trying to remember what else you said.

Executive function skills disorder. Think of the skills required of a CEO—the ability to organize, monitor, and finish things efficiently and effectively. Children with some clusters of learning difficulties lack these skills. Timothy, for example, would start reading his book for a book report, then break off to find a piece of paper for notes, then look at another book, and by the end of writing time have nothing done. Children like Timothy may have amazing amounts of information in their minds but simply not be able to create order out of chaos.

Math problems

Dyscalculia is a difficulty with mathematical symbols and functions. Children with it can't, to varying degrees, grasp simple concepts like addition, subtraction, multiplication, or division. Memorizing math facts is particularly difficult for these children because they see no logic to what they're learning.

Motor problems

Fine motor problems cause children to have difficulty using their hands to perform tasks such as writing or manipulating small objects like Legos or puzzle pieces.

Gross motor problems cause children to have difficulty using their larger muscles for running, jumping, hopping, and so on. Young children with these problems look awkward or clumsy and may often bump into people and things.

Attention problems

These are not, technically speaking, learning disabilities, but they very often occur among children who have learning problems (see pages 35-36). ❏

How Are Learning Disabilities Detected?

Eddie was a precocious preschooler who talked and walked early. But once he started school, his brightness began to fade. About a month after second grade began, his parents received a note from his teacher: "Eddie is becoming more and more of a problem. He rarely pays attention and seems very immature. His work is sloppy and incomplete, and his handwriting is illegible. I'm sure he could do better if he put in more effort. We should talk."

Naturally, his parents were upset—as most of us would be. Before children are identified as having learning disabilities, parents usually get a version of the very negative message Eddie's parents received, usually from a teacher who knows something is wrong, but doesn't know what.

Why teachers don't recognize the problem

Many teachers today are more tuned in to learning disabilities than they used to be, and occasionally they do suggest that a child like Eddie be tested. But more often they act the way Eddie's teacher did—they start using labels like "lazy," "sloppy," and "immature" before the real problem is identified.

Even a well-meaning teacher can misinterpret these problems because the signs of disabilities vary so much from child to child. Poor performance and underachievement in school are common ones, but kids with learning disabilities are frequently inconsistent. Like Eddie, they do well at something one day and poorly at the same thing the next. Sometimes they may seem depressed (can you blame them?) or have difficulty making friends. And often they act out in ways that are very frustrating for teachers to deal with, as Eddie did. Getting into fights, not completing work on time, and handing in sloppy papers are just the sorts of behavior that drive teachers crazy.

Parents can get the ball rolling

Fortunately for Eddie, his parents didn't get caught up in the labels. Their meeting with the teacher led to a gathering of his school's child study team, which included a guidance counselor, school psychologist, administrator, special education teacher, and classroom teacher. Most schools have a similar type of team, but they may call it by a different name.

By the time the meeting was over, everyone agreed that Eddie should be recommended for testing. Educators used to think that learning disabilities didn't show up until around fourth grade. But today they put more emphasis on early detection, believing that the sooner our children get the help they need, the less damage the problems will cause.

Who does the testing?

Sometimes a school psychologist, who is trained to administer most educational and

DID YOU KNOW ?

◆ If your child needs testing and remediation, it's your school district's responsibility to offer it and pay for it. That includes occupational therapy to learn how to use a pencil. Even children who attend private school are entitled to this in the school district in which they pay taxes.

intelligence tests as well as other tests that can detect learning disabilities, can do a fine job of identifying disabilities and making suggestions of how teachers can help. And this testing is free!

But parents aren't always satisfied with these results. Eddie's parents weren't because the results showed that Eddie had superior intelligence but didn't pick up any learning disabilities. "We knew he was bright," said his mom, "but we were sure there had to be some reason he was having so much difficulty. We were determined to find out what it was."

Though standardized tests should produce similar results, some tests, especially psychological ones, depend on a tester's observations, so two different testers can come up with different results for the same child. Sometimes further testing by a specialist is necessary.

Occasionally your school district's committee on special education will agree to pay for any additional testing, but if they don't, it can cost several thousand dollars unless your insurance covers physician-requested testing.

Call in the experts

Eddie's parents followed the steps most experts advise and started with their pediatrician. Why? Learning disabilities are sometimes physiological problems that have to do with the way an individual's

ADVICE FROM KIDS

More survival techniques from kids with learning disabilities:

○ "If you don't know what's going on, wait for the end of the class and talk to the teacher privately," says Jan, 7.

○ "Lay low if other kids are being jerks about your brain. It's best to just stay out of the line of fire," advises Tim, 12.

○ "It gets easier as you get older, so just hang in there however you can," says Adam, 13.

○ "Let people know if you need more time," counsels Greta, 10.

brain functions, and many health insurance policies will cover all or some of the costs—provided that testing is requested by a physician. Although pediatricians don't diagnose learning disabilities, they examine children every day and will know where best to refer you. Eddie's mom was referred first to a neurologist, and then to a neuropsychologist who specialized in testing for learning disabilities and attention deficit hyperactivity disorder (ADHD).

The neuropsychologist was the one who changed Eddie's life at school. Trained to administer very complex tests, neuropsychologists also make educational recommendations to classroom teachers based on the results.

What the tests tell you

As they do for all kids, the tests revealed both Eddie's strengths—he was highly intelligent and very articulate—and his difficulties. Because Eddie's visual and auditory perceptual abilities were at a low level, he had a hard time combining sounds as well as writing—the reason for the sloppy papers. On the one hand Eddie was a good thinker who could talk about what was on his mind; on the other his motor functioning was that of a four-year-old!

"No wonder Eddie had difficulty holding a pencil and putting words on paper," said his parents. "The miracle was that he could do it at all!" No one was surprised to hear

he also had attention deficit disorder (ADD), which made it difficult for him to remain focused on his work—no matter how hard he tried.

Putting the findings to work

After reading the report, the child study team met again and agreed to "classify" Eddie as learning disabled. (Words like "classify" can be terrifying to a parent, but in this case they don't need to be.) This entitled him, as it does in all school districts, to an Individual Educational Plan (IEP)—a plan devised specifically to meet his educational needs.

For Eddie, this meant that his teacher had to give him lots of opportunities to speak in class. The neuropsychologist suggested she praise him for his efforts and for the work he completed, even if it was less work than another student had done, and not make any negative comments about his written work, even if it did look sloppy.

The changes the teacher put into effect paid off in a big way—as they do for most kids with learning differences. For one thing, the more accommodating she tried to be, the more successful Eddie was, and the more successful he was, the more enthusiastic about and interested in school he became. He still moved around a lot, but his behavior was less irritating because his teacher understood it in the context of his disability. ❏

"**H**ere's what it can feel like inside my head," says twelve-year-old Sam. "It's like watching TV with the screen split into about twelve boxes with twelve different shows going on at once. I watch one, then I notice another, and then another." At the same time he feels as though he needs to run or jump or just get his body moving because there's energy inside that has to get out.

Sam, like an estimated five to ten percent of American school-age children, suffers from attention deficit hyperactivity disorder (ADHD). As his parents look back, they realize that he was always an active, impulsive child who ran from the slide to the swing to the treehouse and back again and could never stick with a game for very long, even when playing with his friends.

In fact, the symptoms of ADHD usually show up when kids are between the ages of four and seven, but no one really notices them until a child goes to school and is expected to sit for an extended period of time and focus on a single activity.

The difference between ADD and hyperactivity

In many kids, like Sam, attention deficit disorder (ADD) and hyperactivity appear together. But children can also suffer from only one of the two disorders.

If your child has ADD, he has difficulty focusing and paying attention. If he's hyperactive, he has trouble staying still. "I didn't really think about getting up," says a hyperactive eight-year-old. "My body just did it!" "I wanted to pay attention to what you were saying," a girl with ADD explains, "but there was a truck outside and a dog was walking by."

Until fairly recently experts thought ADD, hyperactivity, and ADHD were problems suffered primarily by boys. Now we know that girls, though less likely to be hyperactive, have ADD as frequently as boys do, but it affects them in a very different way. A boy with ADD might be fidgeting and jumping up and down in his seat. A girl, on the other hand, might drift off quietly without disturbing a soul, the way Clarissa did in third grade. She missed out on half a year's worth of work,

What About Hyperactivity & Attention Deficit Disorder (ADD)?

▶ PARENT TIPS

Jane and Harry, whose daughter has ADD, suggest:

▶ Set up a study area away from distractions.

▶ Ask the teacher to make a checklist of homework and items to be brought to school the next day. Go over the list with your child before bed.

▶ Think in terms of praise and rewards, rather than punishment. These kids already have a lot of negative feedback to deal with.

▶ Maintain a few consistent rules with immediate consequences whenever each rule is broken, and make sure rules are phrased positively.

Ritalin: Pros and Cons

◆ About 3% to 4% of American children take this medication to control hyperactivity. Most of them are boys.

◆ In the short term, it allows kids to concentrate and be more productive, ends aggressive and impulsive behavior, and generally improves academic work. When it works, it can seem like a magic cure.

◆ Long-term benefits to social adjustment, thinking skills, and academic achievement, however, are limited.

◆ The downside includes side effects like sleep problems, slowed growth, tic disorders, and problems with thinking or social interaction, although these can usually be eliminated by reducing the dosage.

◆ Concerns have been raised that the drug is occasionally prescribed inappropriately.

but because she was so quiet, even the teacher didn't notice!

Diagnosing the problem

Diagnosing hyperactivity, ADD, or the combination ADHD is a rather subjective science; there are no tests for it, and experts rely on checklists of symptoms. Just about every parent who reads a list of these will say, "My child acts like this sometimes." The key is that in kids with these disorders the symptoms occur in clusters, and they are extreme enough for you to have an inkling that something is not right.

Symptoms of hyperactivity

These children are always running around or climbing on things. They have difficulty sitting still without fidgeting or even staying seated at all. They move about a great deal during sleep. And, generally, they act as though they're driven by a motor that never shifts into neutral! Usually the symptoms are evident before kids reach the age of seven and have lasted at least six months.

Symptoms of ADD

Kids with ADD have trouble with inattention and impulsivity. What does that really mean?

Inattention. Jeremy was a textbook case of a boy with ADD. In his fourth-grade class he was always humming, drumming his fingers, and looking out the window while his teacher was talking. When she called on him, he never knew what she'd said. He began assignments with gusto, but rarely finished them. During science, his favorite subject, he couldn't seem to concentrate on the water experiments the class was doing. On the playground with his friends, he couldn't stick with a game.

Impulsivity. This is the other part of ADD, and Jeremy had some of these symptoms, too, like acting before thinking, shifting frequently from one activity to another, and having unusual trouble for a fourth grader in organizing his work. Other kids with ADD need to have the teacher at their side to get a job done and call out frequently in class, and they may have a very hard time waiting their turn.

You may be thinking that it's pretty typical for children—particularly preteens—to act without considering the consequences and to have trouble waiting for a turn. The key in deciding if kids have ADD is that they have a cluster of symptoms that fall into the "unusually" and "excessive" categories, like Jeremy. He was very disorganized, but so were half the kids in his fourth-grade class. The fact that he also had other symptoms were indications that the problem was not "usual." If you have an uncomfortable feeling that your child's actions aren't "usual," trust your instincts and follow up with a closer look. ❏

We have a comforting custom in our family of wiping the slate clean with some magic words. After a terrible fight or some especially bad experience, one of my children will inevitably say, "Can we start all over?" And when I say, "Sure," there's a palpable sense of relief.

Unfortunately, parents can't totally wipe the slate clean when their kids have a bad year at school, even though they can do much to help ease the pain. The sad truth is that what happens during a bad year can sometimes cause damage so severe that bits of it will linger and linger. How long often depends on what caused the bad year.

What causes a bad year?

Sometimes it's easy to figure out the reason. Roberta's parents knew sixth grade wasn't going to be a great year when their daughter broke her femur in a water-skiing accident a week before school started and was out of school for two months. Despite a tutor, she dropped behind in schoolwork and, not surprisingly, felt isolated at an age when social involvement is extremely important. In fact, missing school because of recurring illness often results in a bad year.

But sometimes the reasons are more complicated. A year with a bad teacher may destroy a child's desire to learn in school or even convince him that he must be stupid. If a child is the first among her peers to reach puberty, she may be subjected to so much teasing that she simply can't concentrate. A student with undiagnosed learning problems may spend a year wondering why everyone is successful but her.

When our kids' self-esteem and confidence take a beating over an entire year, they can end up feeling that school stinks, that learning is no fun, that they'll never be able to catch up academically, and that they'll never have any friends. Sometimes these memories last a lifetime.

Which years count the most?

One bad year can be particularly devastating if it's kindergarten, first grade, fourth grade, or early in middle school.

Kindergarten and first grade are the years in which children develop a sense of who they are as learners. A first grader who is way behind in reading, for example, may continue to see himself as "slow" long after he's caught up and surpassed his buddies.

Fourth grade is another big shift—kids are learning to use skills to advance their own learning. Marjorie, who was sick for three months, missed so much school that now, in high school, she still has a hard time researching and pulling together information on her own.

A critical part of a middle-school program involves learning the skills that students need to go off and learn on their own. Here again, a child who misses out may feel lost for many years to come.

How to help

Fortunately, the picture is not all doom and gloom. If parents stay alert to their child's behavior and step in and help, a child can compensate for a terrible year, even one of the "critical" ones.

Most important, we can do what comes naturally—keep letting our kids know they're terrific, as Craig's parents did. They knew he was unhappy in first grade because he never talked about school and was having bad dreams. But not until the end of the year did they realize their son had spent every day in a room with someone who had a great deal of power over him and who he knew didn't like him. Qualities that his kindergarten teacher had adored—his enthusiasm and desire to know—were regarded negatively. Although they couldn't wipe out that bad year, his parents made sure that Craig had a teacher the following year who appreciated him.

When we help our kids through a bad year, they come to understand some important truths about life: that not every year will be great; that they'll have good teachers and not-so-good teachers; and that part of getting along in the world is making the best of a situation. Learning they can handle a difficult time is a powerful lesson for our kids. ❑

▶ PARENT TIPS

Ways to compensate for a bad year:

▶ **Focus on strengths.** Pick an area where your child has talent or interest, such as a sport, chess, computers, art, dance, or music, and enroll him in an after-school class with an instructor who will help him feel valuable.

▶ **Don't let 2 bad years happen in a row.** "Fourth grade was a disaster for Mike," says his mom, "so I visited all the 5th-grade classes and requested a particular teacher!"

▶ **Get help when kids need it, whether academic or psychological.** A child may feel embarrassed about having a tutor, but that usually turns into relief. Most children will accept going to a therapist if your message is "We care about how you feel, and this person will help you feel better."

WHAT TO DO
The Best Advice

Clues That Your Child Is Having Problems

When our kids are having trouble at school, it would be great if they could walk into the house, sit down at the kitchen table, and say, "I'm having a hard time because my teacher goes too fast in math. I don't understand long division and feel too embarrassed to ask her to slow down and give me special attention."

Just so you know: this rarely, if ever, happens. The more likely scenario is much more complicated. Like many parents, Sam's mom learned her son was in trouble from his teacher, who phoned because Sam was getting into frequent fights with two boys in his class. Only after several conferences and talks with Sam did she and his teacher come to understand the fights were the result of a bigger school problem. Sam was having so much difficulty with the work in the slowest math group that two smarter boys were teasing him mercilessly. Before you figure out why your child is having trouble, you'll probably first have to deal with other issues that were triggered by the real problem, as Sam's mom did.

What report cards do—and don't—tell you

A poor report card is another way the school alerts parents to their child's school difficulties. Kate's mom was shocked when she brought home straight Cs on her first report card in first grade. What was wrong? The report card didn't say anything about why Kate wasn't doing better. When Kate's mom investigated, it turned out that Kate was having trouble understanding the teacher's directions, something her teacher hadn't realized.

The information we get from our children's report cards is limited—and late in the game. We have to learn to read between the lines and also recognize that since report cards are only issued three or four times a year, a problem may be well entrenched before bad news reaches us. And, as Sam and Kate's moms both discovered, the real reason a child is having difficulty in school may not always be obvious, even to the child's teacher.

Be a detective

Kids sometimes don't understand exactly what's bothering them at school either, and

▶ PARENT TIPS

Other clues to school troubles parents have observed in their kids:

- ▶ Sleep problems and nightmares.
- ▶ Reluctance to go to school.
- ▶ Talking back to the teacher and breaking rules at school.
- ▶ Rudeness, not doing chores, and arguing a lot at home.
- ▶ Self-deprecating remarks like "I'm so stupid" and "I can't do anything right."
- ▶ Sudden changes in friends, grades, school performance, personality, and eating habits.

Getting kids to talk

Once you pick up the trail of clues, you can best hone in on a school problem by getting your child to talk, and, as we all know, that's often a difficult task. Direct questions rarely work. With most kids, the question "Are you having a problem at school?" elicits the answer "No." Experts recommend an indirect approach, with questions like "How is math different this year?" or "What's Mrs. Benedict like as a teacher?"

Listen carefully first and be sensitive to your child's nonverbal signals. If she's fidgeting, won't look at you, or chews on her fingers, she may be trying to tell you, "Slow down—I'm not sure I can tell you everything right now."

No matter what the problem, make sure you let your child know that you're on her side, understand her feelings, and will help her find a way to make things better. Some of the problems that are most painful to children do seem trivial to adults. But the feelings with which your child experiences them are never trivial. A child who is convinced that she's dumb doesn't feel better when her parents tell her that she's smart. She may feel comforted, though, if her mom simply says, "That must be so difficult for you. What can we do to make it easier?" Letting her know there is help to be found is a giant step toward dealing with the actual problem. ❑

if they do, they may be too embarrassed to tell us. So we have to keep alert for those vague clues—like changes in mood and behavior—that let us know something is awry. Getting into fights, the way Sam did, is a common reaction to learning and social problems. Physical complaints are another typical tip-off. The school nurse informed Gillian's mom that Gillian was visiting her office several times a week with a hurt knee or a stomachache. It turned out that Gillian was avoiding one class because the teacher sometimes made sarcastic remarks when a student gave the wrong answer.

Often clues have no apparent connection to the real problem. But until the underlying difficulty is resolved, nothing you do will fix the situation.

ASK THE EXPERTS

Three elementary-school teachers tell how to handle a bad report card:

- "Don't start discussing a bad report card on your way out the door."
- "Try not to sound angry and judgmental—you'll only make the problem worse."
- "Meet with the teacher to pinpoint problems and devise solutions. Include your child so the meeting is a think tank rather than a dump session."
- "Don't offer to pay your child for better grades. That interferes with self-motivation."
- "Keep it in perspective. One bad report card never ruined anyone's life."

When Your Child Acts Up & Other Behavioral Problems

In second grade, Daniel discovered the power of being a class clown. He was particularly adept at mimicking his teacher, belching on cue, and reproducing an awesome range of body sounds while Mrs. Johnson's back was turned. One day, after he interrupted circle time with an especially loud belch, she read him the riot act. And while she did, Daniel crossed his eyes and touched the tip of his nose with his tongue. His classmates thought it was hilarious—Mrs. Johnson did not. That night she called his parents.

What is "acting up"?

Being a class clown is only one of the many ways our children can disrupt a classroom and be a discipline problem. Some kids always seem to get As in classroom behavior, but many don't, and their ways of acting up range from the not-so-dramatic to the dramatic: wisecracks, outbursts in class, talking back to the teacher, mocking the work, breaking school rules, hitting or kicking other kids, and some things teachers and parents haven't even considered—until they've happened. My son once had a detention because he and three of his friends were caught climbing the auditorium walls!

It's useful for parents to develop a realistic sense of proportion about these discipline infractions. After all, cracking a joke in class is not the same as cursing at a teacher.

If your child is involved in hurting others through threats, actions, or mean-spirited teasing, however, it's always serious.

Sort out your own feelings first

Most of us feel worried or angry when a teacher calls to inform us of our child's bad behavior at school. Even though Daniel's dad knew that he himself wasn't the one in trouble, he felt he must have done something wrong as a parent—and was worried the teacher thought so, too. Sometimes parents are annoyed with the teacher, convinced she's being too hard on their child. And sometimes we're ashamed of and furious with our children for acting up. But high emotions usually cloud the issues and often interfere with finding a solution.

Work with the teacher

When a child has been acting up, we have to stop the disruptive behavior and address the problem behind it—in that order. Daniel's parents, for example, needed to put an end to his clowning, but they also had to figure out why their son needed to be the center of attention all the time. Meeting with the teacher is the first step in tackling the issues and mapping out a plan of action.

At a conference, ask the teacher to try to pinpoint when the bad behavior began and whether there's a pattern to when it occurs. Is there anything that seems to trigger it?

AGE FACTOR

Certain kinds of "acting up" are more common at particular ages.

❖ Kindergartners and 1st and 2nd graders are more likely to talk out of turn and act like clowns for their friends' benefit.

❖ Kids in 3rd and 4th grades are more likely to get involved in scuffles.

❖ In middle school, kids' misbehavior is more likely to have a rebellious quality: rudeness to peers, flaunting rules, and talking back to teachers.

Does it seem to be related to problems with specific children? Some kids act up after recess because they have a hard time settling down. If lunch follows reading time, a child who is frustrated by reading problems may act up in the cafeteria.

Daniel's parents and his teacher also discussed recent changes in Daniel's life—he didn't make the A soccer team and his baby brother was starting to talk—that might be connected to his behavior.

Get your child's side of the story

Listen to your child's side of the story before putting any plan into effect. Daniel, for example, complained that his teacher was unfair, and said, "It's not my fault! I can't help it if all my friends think I'm funny! Mrs. Johnson can't take a joke!"

His parents were sympathetic. They told Daniel that they were going to visit his classroom so they had a better sense of his teacher and what went on there. At the same time, though, they were firm. "We told him that we were delighted to have a son with such a terrific sense of humor," explains his dad, "but that he'd have to be funny with his friends after school."

Together they developed a list of when it was okay to be silly at school, such as during recess, and when it was time to be serious, such as during math, and instituted a regular joke night at home when Daniel was welcome to be as funny as he liked.

Set consequences

Work out with the teacher clear guidelines on what kind of behavior is not permitted and what your child could do instead. A child who thinks a rule is unfair, for example, could write a note to the teacher explaining why.

Then agree on a set of consequences both at school and at home if your child doesn't change his behavior. For Daniel, the bottom line was that whenever he caused a problem in school, he would miss the following day's recess and during that time do a job for Mrs. Johnson. At home, until his parents heard from her that Daniel's behavior had improved, he could not watch TV on school nights. Not surprisingly, Daniel made a quick turnaround.

Another solution recommended by many parents is asking the teacher to send home a daily checklist showing whether a child followed classroom rules, such as not hitting anyone. For each rule followed, parents give their child a point or token and when they have a certain number they earn a privilege like watching TV or having a friend over. This lets kids know that their parents will be kept informed about what they do at school and that they will reinforce the school's behavior code.

Experts also suggest that parents do what Daniel's parents did—meet regularly with the teacher to keep lines of communication open.

ADVICE FROM KIDS

Class Clown

○ "It's really cool to know that you can get everyone laughing. But when you start getting into trouble for making everyone laugh, kids don't really like you so much because they think you might get them into trouble, too. Then you need to stop," says Mike, 10.

Dr. David Anderegg, a psychologist, suggests parents keep these points in mind:

• Remember it's a child's behavior that's at issue—not his character or yours.
• Address the behavior with clear, straightforward consequences, such as, "No weekday playdates until we get a positive report."
• Reward improvements in behavior as in, "Mr. Giles says you've made an effort to stop talking back in class. Why don't we go bowling to celebrate the improvement!"
• Talk to your child and the teacher about possible sources of frustration, both academic and social.

Address reasons for acting up

For many kids, like Daniel, acting up is a way of getting attention. But for some kids, acting up in class is a way of concealing the fact that they don't understand some part of a lesson. Kids who are rude to a teacher or strike other kids may be angry about something else that's going on in their lives. And children who damage school property or steal from other kids may feel that they'll never get the things they need. Sometimes when a child acts up in school, it signals a learning problem with emotional spillovers.

Daniel's parents thought that one reason he was so hungry for attention at school was that everyone spent a great deal of time at home laughing at his little brother's antics. They made it a point to tell him, after they'd put the baby to bed, what a pleasure it was to have some time alone with their "big" kid, and they also spent time doing things with him that the baby could not do, such as building complicated Lego models and playing board games.

Reinforce the positive

We often forget that positive reinforcement for good behavior is just as important as negative consequences for disruptive behavior. A simple comment such as "You showed so much self-control today when your little sister was bugging you" or "You remembered our family rule about not talking back" has a great carryover effect on classroom behavior! Many families have found that putting up a rule chart at home and praising children when they follow those rules helps children establish the habit of thinking about rules and abiding by them. ❑

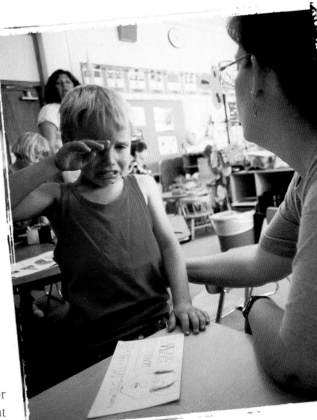

"**M**rs. Sawyer is so unfair. She always calls on Lisa and Miranda, and she never calls on me!"

"I hate Mr. Gould. He's so mean. He embarasses me in front of everyone."

"Mrs. Jackson doesn't know how to take a joke. She's always jumping on me for stuff that's no big deal!"

Most parents hear similar complaints about their kids' teachers at least every now and then. How seriously should we take them? It all depends. Sometimes children grumble about teachers in very much the same way they do about parents— which isn't so surprising. After all, teachers, like parents, are the ones who make kids do all those things they'd really rather not do, like sit quietly while someone else is talking, or rewrite a story that seemed "perfect," or study every single week for a spelling test on Friday.

But when the complaints go on and on and take a tone that says, "My teacher really doesn't like or value me," or "My teacher thinks I'm stupid," we have to take them very seriously and take action. Kids do not do their best work if they are not getting along with the teacher.

Is it bad chemistry—or more?

Teachers are people, too, with different personalities, styles, and ways of doing things that aren't always a good match with our kids. There may be any one of a number of reasons why your child is having trouble with a teacher, and to help, you need to know what it is.

Does the teacher have a style of teaching or maintaining order that simply doesn't work well for everyone? Teachers who yell, for example, may upset kids who come from very quiet homes. A child who does best in an environment with a clear structure may run into difficulties with a teacher whose unstructured classroom requires more self-direction. Maybe the problems are a matter of bad chemistry—a child with a very good sense of humor who is always joking may rub a teacher with no sense of humor the wrong way.

The truth is, though, that some teachers are simply not wonderful, like the one Jake had in third grade. Mrs. Jackson clearly preferred girls and regarded boys as rowdy and messy, responding regularly to their high level of energy by humiliating them for actions another teacher would probably have taken in stride. Jake's mom, Mira, finally realized how bad things were when Jake did an imitation of his teacher one evening at dinner. In a very prissy voice he said, "Jake thinks he's making a joke, class, doesn't he? But we all know there's a difference between being really funny and just being stupid." Mira could hear the rage in Jake's voice as he continued, "And we all know there's a difference between being a teacher and being a total jerk!"

When There's A Problem With A Teacher

ASK THE EXPERTS

What if nothing works?

Dr. Susan Engel, a professor of developmental psychology at Bennington College, advises, "Unfortunately, there are times when you just can't make any inroads with a teacher who is making your child miserable. If that happens, first talk to the principal about the problem, and if that doesn't result in classroom changes, don't hesitate to ask about having your child's teacher changed."

45

ADVICE FROM KIDS

○ "One year I had a teacher that didn't like me no matter what I did. But the year before I had a teacher who loved me. So I stopped by to see her a lot after school. It made me remember that I wasn't such a bad kid!" says Amanda, 5th grade.

○ "My 2nd-grade teacher made jokes that hurt my feelings. Like, once I told her that I went to Disneyland and in front of everyone she said, 'Well bully for you,' and I felt like a jerk. My mom and dad met with her for a conference. She made mean jokes much less after that," explains James, 3rd grade.

Offer sympathy and reassurance

Because Mira could see how upset her son was, the first thing she did was what most of us would do—reassure him. "I want to make school better for you," she said, "but I'll need your help." That evening, she compiled a detailed list of Jake's run-ins with and complaints about his teacher.

Before you arrange a meeting, it sometimes helps to get a reality check on your child's perceptions. Spending an hour or so actually observing the class yourself is a good way, though you can expect the teacher to be more restrained.

Meet with the teacher

Being an advocate for your child and also being respectful of the teacher's authority isn't always easy. Keep in mind that your goal in meeting with the teacher is to build a better relationship between your child and his teacher, not to make them adversaries (see pages 76-78). Strategize. Think about the impact of your words. "My impulse was to go in and be furious," Mira admits, "but I knew that wouldn't help. Instead I tried to figure out a way to make her my ally."

In the end, she shared some important facts about her son with Mrs. Jackson and told her, "Jake wants desperately to please you, but he's not sure how. I'd be happy to work with him. Do you have any suggestions about how he could improve?"

This is a tack that often works well. Most teachers love it when parents offer support. Jake's teacher felt touched, rather than attacked, praised his abilities, and talked about her classroom expectations. In the process Mira came to understand Jake's teacher better, see her son from the teacher's point of view, and learned several ways Jake could improve their relationship. In her follow-up note to Mrs. Jackson, Mira mentioned several of those suggestions. From then on,

the teacher made much more effort in class to find good things in Jake.

When kids won't perform for a teacher

In junior high, another type of problem often crops up: many students start gearing their class performance to how they feel about a teacher. Janet, for example, received a C in science even though she received high grades in her other subjects. Mr. Gould, she claimed to her dad, was "boring and mean." Janet's dad agreed that her teacher was very difficult and listened sympathetically. But he also knew that to succeed in school, his daughter had to develop the ability to work with teachers she didn't particularly like.

Parents can help older kids like Janet learn to communicate their concerns to their teachers. One key is helping them figure out different ways of framing questions: "How can I do this differently?" is likely to be more effective than, "What do you want from me?"

But if a student has made a genuine effort to work things out for herself to no avail, schedule a conference and take on the role of translator between the teacher and your child.

Teaching kids to cope

Kids can learn much from a year with a less-than-perfect teacher. For one thing, they can learn how to build a relationship with someone they find difficult. Janet's dad, for example, suggested she start bringing in interesting science articles she'd clipped from the newspaper. When she did, she discovered her "boring and mean" teacher became much more enthusiastic about her.

Mira helped Jake have a not-so-bad year by talking to him about how to get along with Mrs. Jackson even if she wasn't as wonderful as the teacher he had in second grade. They practiced at home until he could sit back and remind himself not to react to every dig. His mom also helped him notice which kinds of behavior irked his teacher most—calling out in a loud voice, having a messy desk and papers, cracking jokes. He learned to become neater and save his jokes for his dad. And Mira phoned his teacher regularly to see how Jake was doing. By June Jake knew that he could emerge from an uncomfortable situation with both feet firmly planted.

Our kids can also learn that flattery has its place and develop a sense of how far they can go with a particular teacher without causing problems. When my own children have problems with teachers, I usually don't worry as long as I feel that I can talk to the teacher and support my children at home. After all, some of what's lacking in a less-than-perfect teacher can be made up by mom and dad! ❏

AGE FACTOR

❖ It's not unusual for 1st and 2nd graders to fall in love with their teachers. You're liable to hear very frequently how much better he or she does things than you do. This happens less as kids grow older, but 5th graders—on the cusp of adolescence—can still develop a big crush on a teacher.

❖ Sometimes we get jealous of a teacher our child adores. But even one such "love affair" can carry a kid through many rough spots in the years ahead.

When Your Child Can't Get Along With Other Kids

Maria had never been particularly outgoing, but her mom was surprised when the first-grade teacher called to discuss her worries about Maria's social development. It turned out that Maria was always alone and didn't seem to know how to make friends. Her mom became worried, too.

In sixth grade Charlie came home, burst into tears, and told his parents, "I hate school. Everyone teases me." He was in so much pain that his parents felt terrible.

When parents think about learning in school, they usually focus on academics, but the lessons our kids learn about how to survive, and thrive, in a group are every bit as important and enduring.

All kids have problems with others from time to time, but some, like Charlie and Maria, have more trouble than others—and when the problems are significant enough, they interfere with social and academic development. Children who feel isolated and vulnerable often aren't willing to take the risks learning involves: raising a hand and offering answers, joining in group projects, telling stories during circle time, finding a lab partner and working cooperatively. Getting along with others can mean the difference between school being a happy place and a daily torture.

When, over a period of time, a child consistently has problems connecting with other kids at school, gets into fights, or is the subject of constant teasing, experts say that's cause for concern. Parents need to figure out why and find a way to help.

Finding the reason

Most psychologists agree that the first clue to unraveling the problem is when it started. If trouble with peers begins in the very early years of school, its origins, they say, may lie in a lack of social experience. Maria, for example, had not attended preschool and didn't really know how to approach other kids. She also felt anxious about doing anything new—like making friends—with her mom out of sight.

Sometimes parents discover, much to their dismay, that a child's social difficulties correlate with stress at home. That was the case with Joey, who started getting into fights soon after his dad lost his job.

Other reasons have more to do with a lack of social skills. Does your child know how to compromise and negotiate? Is she always bossy? Does he act immature compared with his classmates? Or perhaps your child's aggressiveness has developed into bullying.

Feeling excluded

For middle schoolers, feeling left out seems to be a major part of the curriculum. As they struggle to figure out who they are and where they fit in, peer relationships become almost more important than schoolwork. Because they feel so shaky about their identities, our kids often try to make themselves feel more secure by dumping on others. Carlos, for example, was the ringleader in teasing Charlie, the class brain. "He's a dork," Carlos explained. "All of my friends think so, too!"

The fact that this kind of teaming up and exclusion is par for the developmental course doesn't mean that it isn't painful for the child who is the victim, as Charlie was. Nor does it mean that Carlos' behavior should be passed off as normal.

Enlist the help of teachers

Because teachers see the same social problems year after year, they are often adept at setting up situations in the classroom to help a child socially. Maria's teacher put Maria and another shy girl in charge of several classroom jobs where they had to work together—and they became friends. Teachers can also keep you informed about what they observe in the classroom. Kids with overwhelming social woes often have undiagnosed learning disabilities or suffer from depression, for example.

Beyond that, many middle schools address these social problems as part of the curriculum by assigning books that deal with the issues, talking about them in class, and having kids write about them in journals. After discussing Charlie's problems with his parents, his English teacher decided to have the class read a story about teasing and held a discussion on how that made kids feel.

How to help young children

Home is an ideal place for children to develop better friendship skills. Sometimes young children are overwhelmed by the number of kids in a classroom, and short playdates at home with one classmate at a time are easier for them to manage. For children who get into conflicts, structured activities, like baking cookies or playing a game, are good choices. If you keep an ear to the ground when your child has a friend over, you'll be able to intervene if you hear the beginnings of a problem.

How to help middle schoolers

When our middle schoolers feel left out and different, we can help them find kindred spirits outside of school. If your child is a computer "nerd," as Charlie was, search out an after-school computer program where he'll meet others who share the same interests. A student orchestra may provide friends for a budding violinist. Investigate summer camps that offer activities your child is interested in—friends made there can get a child through a bad year on home ground. It's also important not to underestimate the power of one good friend. Not everyone was born to be part of a pack, and research shows that a child with one good friend will do fine. ❑

When Your Child Says School Is Boring

"**H**ow was school today, honey?" Groans accompany the response: "Oh, Mom, school is just so-oo-oo boring." If you're like many parents, nothing is quite as effective at setting a fire under you as hearing the boredom complaint. Often, our knee-jerk reaction is to blame the school for not providing our child with sufficiently challenging work.

But in my house, as in others, what children mean when they say that school is boring may be very different from what I think it means. Explains Ursula Ferro, retired head of the Lower School at Green Acres School in Rockville, Maryland, "When children complain of boredom they're often saying that they aren't connecting with what's going on in school." Our task, as parents, is to figure out what their complaint means, why they aren't connecting, and help them reconnect.

What "school is boring" can mean

For my friend's daughter, Beth, a third grader, it meant that school was difficult. When she didn't understand a lesson, she drifted off into her imagination instead of working harder, then came home and told her mom how boring school was. "It took a while for me to realize that school was boring because Beth's mind was off in outer space!" says her mom.

Young children who are learning to read sometimes say they're bored when the method used to teach reading doesn't work for them. Older children may complain "math is boring" because they feel lost and therefore disengaged—in much the same way many adults, including me, would feel listening to a lecture on astrophysics.

Children also complain of boredom when they've missed a critical piece of whatever it is they're studying. Think how boring a movie is if you miss the beginning and don't understand what's going on until the very end. A child who has been out sick may find it difficult to reconnect upon his or her return. If you ask, "How was your first day back at school?" you're liable to hear, "Boring!" Translation: "I felt totally out of it socially and besides, they started

► **PARENT TIPS**

► "My daughter was bored because she loves exploring things in-depth. In school they only spent a week on whales, so she and I embarked on a year-long whale project at home. We traveled to aquariums, established Internet relationships with whale watchers in Africa and New Zealand, and whenever she's bored we dig in and learn more," says Alan, father of 3.

► "We simply banned the B word in our house. Our kids can complain all they want about their teachers or the work, and even about hating school. I said that I was bored with the word 'boring.' Ever since, I've heard a lot more information about school," reports Jim, father of 2.

fractions while I was sick so I didn't understand anything during math."

Social, emotional, or even run-of-the-mill growing-up problems can be enough to distract a child from what's happening on the blackboard. It should come as no surprise that the B word is most often heard during the middle-school years when hormones are raging and social concerns become consuming.

Get a translation from your kids

Asking open-ended, but pointed, questions about school is the way you're most likely to find out what "school is boring" means. What was the most interesting thing you learned about in social studies? What was the hardest thing about math? Who was the meanest teacher this week?

Listen first. Often kids need to talk for a while before the reason they're not feeling connected pops out. If you think back to your own school days, you'll probably remember a time when you felt very much the way your kids do right now.

Helping kids reconnect

Once you understand what "boring" means, you'll have a better idea how to help. Sometimes just listening to how kids feel is enough. At other times reassurance that they'll be back in the swim in a few days is needed. Explaining some simple fact about adding fractions may help end math

confusion, but if your child is behind, lost, or having serious social problems, set up a conference with the teacher.

When kids need more challenges

Finally, "boring" can mean what so many of us assume that it means. To determine whether your child needs more stimulating work, look closely at the work he or she is doing in school now and enlist the aid of the teacher, as Andy's dad did after several weeks of complaints about "boring math" from his third-grade son. Mrs. Eisen was pleased to hear Andy was bored. The very next day she told him that because he was capable of much more advanced work in math, she would give him increasingly more difficult work if he did his regular assignments carefully and completely. That strategy gave Andy an incentive to do a good job on the easy work, but also kept pace with his capabilities.

Unfortunately, as many parents know, not all teachers are this receptive. Then we have to look for ways to challenge our kids outside of school. Check out after-school activities, both in school and in the community, as well as summer programs in a subject area your child is interested in, such as music, a foreign language, or computers. Chess clubs, math competitions, dance, martial arts, theater, and all kinds of sports activities are critical for kids who aren't getting "enough" in school. ❏

ASK THE EXPERTS

Ursula Ferro, retired head of the Lower School at Green Acres School in Rockville, Maryland, outlines 5 steps for parents:

• **Trust your own knowledge of your child and your sense that something is or is not wrong.**
• **Find out from your child what he or she means by "boring."**
• **Find out if your child is going through a hard time by asking open-ended questions. Let her know there are people who can help.**
• **Check out the work your child is actually doing.**
• **Ask the teacher to observe your child and let you know what's going on.**

When Your Child Doesn't Want To Go To School

Every child, at some point or another, wants to play hooky from school. I'm convinced that children, like adults, are entitled to an occasional day off from the pressures of the "daily grind." Many parents I know agree, such as the friend I called recently in the middle of the afternoon. To my surprise, her ten-year-old, Joanie, answered. "Are you sick?" I asked. "No," she replied. "I'm just having a mental illness day." I heard her mother yelling in the background, "Mental health! It's a mental health day!"

There's a big range in kids' reluctance to attend school. At one end of the I-don't-want-to-go-to-school spectrum is a child like Joanie, who begs for a "mental health" day every now and then, and at the other is a child like six-year-old Emily, who complains of stomachaches every morning so she can stay home. Her worried mom dragged her to the doctor, but he found nothing physically wrong with Emily. She was suffering from a malady that hits a surprising number of kids at some time in their school career: school phobia. For these kids the problem goes on and on unless parents take firm steps to end it.

Typical symptoms

Sometimes children who are developing a phobia about school are very direct, as in: "I don't want to go." But often they complain about headaches or stomachaches, as Emily did, or say they feel faint. In school they may spend a lot of time in the nurse's office. Rule out any actual physical cause first by checking with your pediatrician. If nothing is wrong, find out the reason behind the classroom phobia and address it.

Why kids develop school phobia

There are several common causes. Among younger children and kids who are starting in a new school, it's usually a form of separation anxiety—a fear about leaving their parents. A teacher who yells occasionally or an incident at school may trigger or aggravate the anxiety, but the real problem is the anxiety itself. Sometimes it starts during the first week of school, especially with kindergartners. Not all five-year-olds are ready to skip off without looking back, and some kids need extra preparation and reassurance to be comfortable on their own. Many parents don't realize that some children also have a hard time returning to school after a vacation or bout of illness.

Worries about separation may also be related to a problem or change at home. Emily loved first grade until her baby brother was born. Justin's reluctance to attend school coincided with his parents' separation and his dad moving out— he felt he had to stick around or some other terrible thing would happen. Six-year-old Elena, whose mom was caring for a Grandma with Alzheimer's disease, was worried something might happen to her mom while she was at school.

For older children in second, third, and fourth grades, the biggest cause of school phobia is a learning problem like attention deficit disorder, which makes school an ongoing source of frustration. Seven-year-old Caleb, who suffered from ADD, did fine in an unstructured kindergarten, but by second grade, where the expectations were more rigorous, he had become increasingly anxious about school—and wanted to stay home.

Children rarely develop school phobia when they enter middle school. If they do, social issues are usually at the heart of it. To a child who feels as though no one likes him, staying home and sleeping looks like an attractive alternative to coping with being "out" at school. Specific situations, such as a bully on the playground, can also inspire reluctance to attend school.

The best solutions

While it's important to be sympathetic to a child who is frightened about school, experts agree that letting your child stay home beyond a day or two is not the solution. Every day a child isn't in school only reinforces the anxiety and the idea that there is something to be afraid of. But simply taking a child to the classroom and leaving him is not the answer, either.

Once you've figured out the cause, you can take steps to help your child in ways that make sense. A kindergartner may need a parent to stay at the back of the classroom for the first few days. One mom realized long good-byes and saying, "I'll miss you," were making her daughter more anxious. Emily's mom set aside a special time for her after school to let her know she was just as important as the new baby. Justin's dad called him after school from work. And Elena's teacher worked out a plan for her to call home during recess.

When older children are frightened about going to school or the problem is a bully, experts urge parents to involve the school right away and to maintain very close contact with the teacher. If there is any evidence of a learning problem, have your child tested (see pages 70-71 and 32-34). Kids with school phobia in middle school often need help from a school counselor. ❑

▶ PARENT TIPS

▶ "I put notes in J.P.'s lunch box that say, 'Hi! I'm thinking about you and hope you're having a great day. See you soon!' It gives him a little boost for the second half of his day when he's feeling homesick," says his mom.

▶ "I gave Anthony my special Yankee cap to keep in his locker. When he feels lonely at rest time, he smells my cap!" explains his dad.

▶ "To help Carol go it alone the second week of kindergarten, we taped a picture of our family, including the dog, in her cubby," offers her mom.

If The Problem Is Schoolwork

There it was in black and white on David's report card. According to his teacher, his poor grades were caused by his lack of motivation, poor work habits, and plenty of just not paying attention in class. Some children who do poorly in schoolwork are like David: in order to improve their writing, math, reading, or social studies work, they first need help with more general learning skills.

Others have learning or emotional problems that interfere with their abilities to absorb facts, to concentrate, or to do well in certain subjects.

Still others are like Nancy's daughter, Kerri, who is well-adjusted and likes school, but as her mom says, "just doesn't do very well when it comes to the actual work, like memorizing the multiplication tables, analyzing the parts of speech, or writing a story—even though testing ruled out learning and emotional problems."

If your child needs help to become more motivated and improve his work habits, like David, or learn how to do better in one or more subjects, like Kerri, you may need to look for various solutions.

Team up with the teacher

Once you know what part of schoolwork your child is struggling with, you can work together with the teacher to discuss options for help and map out a plan to improve the situation that you, the teacher, and your child can all agree on. Try to come away from a meeting with a list of specific goals for your child, a sense of what kind of help he or she needs, and an arrangement for progress reports from the teacher. One of David's goals was paying more attention in class. To help him do that, his teacher agreed to change his seat so that it was right in front of the chalkboard and to touch his shoulder gently whenever she saw he was drifting off.

Often even a small change or different approach can make the difference. Kerri's math improved once her teacher had her

▶ **PARENT TIPS**

"This 5-point plan worked for us," says an Ohio mom:

▶ Develop an improvement contract with your child and the teacher, put it in writing, and have everyone sign it. Include daily homework times and reading expectations.

▶ Help your child get organized. That means clearing out a drawer for pens, pencils, and paper, investing in an assignment pad, checking that backpacks are packed at night, and whatever else might help.

▶ Set rules and consequences. Instead of nagging, remind your child of the rules: "I'm sorry you decided not to finish studying. That means you have also decided not to let yourself talk on the phone." Be consistent.

▶ Ask teachers to send home a weekly report.

▶ Don't demand perfection. Encourage effort and praise each bit of improvement, even if it's small.

work in a small group instead of alone. A child who seems terribly disorganized may rapidly start doing better when a teacher checks his assignment books every day to make sure things are written down.

Many teachers are willing to stay after school occasionally to coach students individually. Since children are often embarrassed to ask for this, set it up with the teacher yourself. Teachers who can't work with a child are usually happy to meet with parents to help them learn how to help their child. Let's face it: we don't always know how to coach our kids.

Check out tutoring

Some kids need the more extensive help of a regular tutoring routine.

Learning centers. More and more schools are starting their own after-school homework centers, but if your child's school doesn't have one, a number of learning-center chains now exist that help kids with specific subjects, organizational skills, and study habits. But before you sign up, make sure you know precisely what the center's agenda is and how it meshes with your needs. Some want to put kids through a series of tests to see where their academic "holes" are; others are very focused on learning styles. Talk to families whose kids have attended to help you assess whether or not it's a good match for your child.

Peer tutoring. Middle schools often have peer-tutoring programs in which students who excel in a specific area help others. Frequently older kids tutor younger ones, but in some programs children in the same grade help one another. The programs that work best take the stigma out of "not knowing" by stressing the fact that we all have strengths and weaknesses. A student who offers tutoring in math may require tutoring from a peer in history. However, this kind of tutoring can easily become

just a social event, so make sure that you—or the teacher—check periodically to see that learning is taking place!

Hiring a tutor. Many parents resist this idea, but they shouldn't. Tutors can be expensive, but a good one will probably teach himself out of a job fairly quickly. And while many parents, like Kerri's mom, plan to tutor their children themselves, they often come to recognize that they don't have the temperament for it. After a week of battles Kerri's mom gave up. "I was impatient and short-tempered," she admits. "Kerri and I just yelled about commas instead of the mess in her room." Although Kerri was mortified to have a tutor, as many kids are, the tutor's systematic plan—first reviewing everything from the week that had just ended, then previewing what was coming up—made her feel very confident in class. And her grades improved.

Other ways to help

Traditional types of school-based help aren't always the answer. Sometimes our kids soak up information better in other ways.

Enrichment. In the fourth grade my friend's son was studying the solar system and just couldn't seem to grasp how moons spun around planets and planets spun around the sun while they were rotating on their own axis. His dad decided a visit to a nearby planetarium was in order, and

after two days of films and hands-on exhibits he had absorbed several weeks' worth of science material.

Trips to historical recreations such as Williamsburg or Sturbridge Village reinforce what children have studied in history; seeing or acting in a Shakespearean play changes it into something more than archaic language on a densely packed page. These kinds of visits make learning come alive for all kids but are especially important for children who learn best visually.

Computer programs. Sometimes children can find the one-on-one help they need by using a fun learning program on a computer. Memorizing math facts was my own son's nemesis until we bought a CD-ROM called *Math Workshop* (see page 96). Suddenly memorizing times tables was a game, and he didn't want to stop playing. There are hundreds of comparable skill-driven programs that teach everything from vocabulary to problem solving.

Children with learning disabilities often do especially well with these programs. For one thing, they enable them to proceed at their own pace, without risking humiliation among peers. For another, many kids who have difficulty writing with a pencil are liberated when they learn keyboarding skills. And finally, children who have a hard time focusing their attention on the printed page often respond well to the lively graphics and sounds of CD-ROMs. ❑

For most parents, the number one concern about their child's schoolwork is reading. If our kids haven't yet learned how, we're worried about why they haven't and when they should begin. If they have, we ask ourselves, "When should I assume that my child has a problem?" or "Why is my child such a slow reader?"

Actually, parents are right to worry about reading because it's the cornerstone of all learning. There is nothing our children do in school that they won't do better if they're good readers—and that includes math, science, technology, and even sports.

Why kids have trouble

Many educators now believe two things about learning to read: some children have trouble because the approach being used doesn't work for them; others who are unusually slow in developing reading skills may have learning disabilities.

For students like Eve's daughter, Kim, who had made no progress in reading by the end of first grade, the problem was the "whole-language" approach to teaching reading used in many schools nationwide. Consider this fact: between 1988, when California began using this approach, and 1994, the reading scores of that state's students declined from the middle of the nation's scores to last place, and sixty percent of the state's fourth-grade students couldn't read at a basic level!

Eve and other parents and educators blamed the whole-language approach because it doesn't teach phonics—the process of learning to sound out words and letter combinations. Reading is a process of decoding symbols, explains Dr. Bill Honig, former California superintendent of schools, and until you comprehend the symbols and learn a decoding method, you can't read. He says, "It's like trying to play baseball without being taught how to hit." As Eve discovered, some children, like Kim, also need to be taught several different ways to grasp the relationship between sounds and letters.

What you need to know

Don't assume that your children will eventually learn to read "naturally" without training in reading skills. Experts now agree that by the middle of first grade children should be reading simple sentences and decoding simple words, such as "red" or "big." Though the usual age range for beginning to read is five to seven, by the time children finish third grade they should read at grade level and understand what they've read.

To determine how well your children read now, ask them to read aloud from a school reading book and answer questions to see if they comprehend what they've read. If your children can't do those things, time will not cure their problems.

About Reading Problems

DID YOU KNOW?

◆ About 20% of all children have difficulty learning to read phonetically, which is a good predictor of reading disabilities. It can best be overcome with a series of awareness exercises that include phonics, rhyming games, and rhythmic clapping games that accentuate syllables in words.

◆ Of the 4th graders evaluated in 39 states for the National Assessment of Educational Progress (NAEP), 40% failed to demonstrate even a basic understanding of what they read.

While very few schools still use only the whole-language approach, ask your child's teacher how he or she teaches reading. What approach does the school use? Does it include systematic lessons in phonics skills and phonemic awareness—what the letters and their combinations sound like? Does it use both aural and visual reading exercises? Don't panic if the school uses bits of a whole-language program. Its emphasis on reading first-rate children's literature continues to be important.

How does your child learn?

Some children seem able to learn to read by just about any method, but many can't. If you share information about the way you think your child learns with the teacher, he or she can adapt a reading program so it works. Kim's mother remembered how Kim had learned the words of nursery rhymes after hearing them only once or twice. Not surprisingly, Kim also remem-bered words best after hearing letter combinations. For other children, looking at words and letter combinations is most important, and still others require a multisensory approach.

If the teacher is resistant to tailoring a reading program to meet your child's needs, and he or she is not reading at the appropriate level for the grade, bring your concerns to the principal. If you're still not satisfied, call the National Right to Read Foundation (1-800-468-8911) for an at-home phonics test to help assess your child's ability and the best home instruction programs available.

There are some children who simply don't learn to read even when every effort is made to match their learning style with a reading program. They need to be tested for reading disabilities (see pages 32-34).

What else can parents do?

Most parents aren't surprised to hear that studies show kids are more likely to become good readers when parents read aloud to them. Those who love to read remember the good feeling of sitting on a parent's lap night after night hearing stories. Our kids' similar feelings spill over on how they regard reading in school. We can also pay very close attention to the kind of progress our children are making with reading and ask the teacher for ideas of games and activities that reinforce the skills without sapping the pleasure from reading. ❏

► **PARENT TIPS**

► "We hold a nightly living room reading party for half an hour. Everyone—including my husband and I—brings a book," says Melinda, mother of 3.

► "We take turns reading aloud at night. So far, favorites are *Stuart Little* and an old Bobbsey twins book from Grandma's attic," says Andrea, mother of 4.

Math is the second major area of study during elementary and middle school, and it involves a different kind of thinking than reading and language do. A surprising number of our children—even very smart ones—have difficulties with math during these years. These can range from trouble memorizing math facts to the serious math anxiety that Kathryn, an eighth-grade honors student in everything but math, feels. "I see numbers and symbols on a page," she says, "and I panic."

Some parents, who consider themselves bad-at-math people, feel the same anxiety when they think about trying to help their kids overcome problems with math. No wonder mathematics creates more home-work strife than any other school subject!

Why kids have trouble

In the early grades, math is basic arithmetic: adding, subtracting, multiplying, and dividing. What that boils down to is lots of memorizing math facts and times tables. Kids who have math problems in kindergarten through second grade usually have a hard time with memorization or with paying attention to the kind of detail that's required for math facts. "What's six times three?" I asked my son in second grade. "Seventeen," he said after some thinking. "No," I said, "it's eighteen." He smiled broadly and replied, "I was real close!" In math, that's not close enough!

By third and fourth grade math becomes more abstract, with problems like this one: A train leaves the station at 10:00 in the morning and is traveling at eighty miles per hour. If it's going to a town two hundred miles away, what time will it arrive? Now students need to be able to read carefully, analyze, and figure out how to solve the problem, and for some of them this shift from more concrete and straightforward basic arithmetic is difficult.

At this stage, pinpointing precisely why children are having trouble may require some investigation. Are they poor readers who didn't actually understand the problem? Do they know how to analyze and imagine possible ways of tackling the problem? Do they lack confidence? Even though they can rattle off their multiplication tables on cue, that doesn't mean they know when they need to divide and when they need to multiply.

What about math anxiety?

Students such as Kathryn, who are generally confident, sometimes have one very specific pocket of fear, and often it's math. As soon as she senses a math problem coming, Kathryn freezes. The more problems she gets wrong, the more desperate she becomes; and the more desperate she becomes, the less able she is to think. By the time she was in fourth grade, she'd labeled herself a "bad-at-math kid."

About Math Problems

ADVICE FROM KIDS

○ "I practice math by cooking with my mom. There's lots of measuring, and sometimes I have to figure out how to double a recipe," says Ellen, 9.

○ "My dad asks me to figure out what percent of my allowance I spend on food each week! It's a lot!" reports Dan, 12.

○ "Adding is easy for me now, because my family plays Scrabble every night, and I keep score," explains Alex, 8.

In fact, math is the only area of the school curriculum that has an identifiable "phobia" connected to it. What causes it? Psychologist Dr. Janet Weisberg speculates, "If you have to write a paragraph, everyone knows there will be all sorts of right ways to do it, and that makes it fun to experiment. But when it comes to math, we all think in terms of a right and a wrong answer, and that makes everyone nervous."

Good-at-math kids instinctively seem to know, as good math teachers do, that math is not just about right and wrong answers but is really about the process of searching for answers and relationships.

Finding the joy in math

How do you help a bad-at-math kid get over his problems and discover how much fun math can be? That depends on what his problem is.

If you have a young (or older) child who's having difficulty memorizing math facts, make drills at home into games. One mother picks a number every morning and relates everything at breakfast to that number—she serves each person seven little pancakes, seven tiny glasses of juice, seven blueberries, and so on—so practicing math facts becomes fun. Sheila's dad taught her to add like a machine by playing Five Hundred Rummy for a half-hour each evening. "Sheila always had to add up her points, and I showed her that the fastest

way was to make groups of ten. The more cards we played, the faster she added. After a while there were no problems." Any math practice related to money generally motivates kids. Ask them to add the prices of two candy bars or toys, pay the cashier, and figure out what the change should be.

Learning from good-at-math kids

You also need to help kids discover the pleasures of problem solving—which is where kids who love math instinctively begin—and teach them to visualize problems, rather than to try to memorize approaches and formulas.

Sometimes it helps to use actual things. If you're talking about apples and oranges, get some apples and oranges. When you talk about a pie graph, bring out a pie. My younger son, who is not a math whiz, had a very hard time in third grade understanding that one-quarter was smaller than one-third. After all, four is a bigger number than three, so why wasn't one-quarter bigger?

Then my older son, who is the family math whiz, told him how to visualize the problem: "Nat," he said, "if you had a brownie that you really loved, would you rather split it into four pieces and share it with three friends, or split it into three pieces and share it with two friends?" "Ohhh," Nat said, light dawning. "Maybe you shouldn't have any friends over," Noah added. "We can just split it in half!"

Getting comfortable with numbers

There are many opportunities for children to use numbers and problem solving at home. Calculating how long it will take to get to grandma's house, figuring out what fifteen percent of a restaurant check comes to, adding up how much three desired toys will cost, and dividing the number of cookies on a plate equally are daily math problems that we can work on with kids. For ideas on how everyday things can be viewed as math problems, read a funny children's book, *Math Curse* (see page 92).

Once children have developed the confidence to tackle problems, they usually have far fewer math troubles at school. These solutions work well for children with math anxiety, too. As with any fear, engineering successful experiences leads to more success.

Math and learning disabilities

Although most kids who struggle with math don't have learning disabilities, experts agree that if a child is plagued by math problems and standard remediation doesn't work, it's a good idea to have the child tested (see pages 32-34). ❏

If Your Child Does Poorly On Tests

ASK THE EXPERTS

Psychologist Dr. Janet Weisberg explains:

• "Kids who are invested in being successful feel an enormous amount of pressure when they take a test because they feel that their identity is at stake. 'What will happen if I don't succeed?' That adds to their sense of panic. As they learn to define 'success' in broader terms, they'll feel less anxiety about tests."

"Gerry starts studying for a big test at least a week ahead," says his dad. "I go over everything with him until I'm convinced that he really knows his stuff. But he ends up with a C or D anyway. Now he just expects to screw up!"

"Every Friday Lisa has a spelling test," says her mom. "I see her going over the list of twenty-five words, but something about the way she's studying must be wrong, because when she takes the test, she misses at least five of them!"

Does your child suffer from one of the test problems that these worried parents are describing, or a different one entirely? Many kids do. Even though they put in the studying effort, when they take the test, something goes wrong.

Why do kids have trouble with tests?

Some kids do poorly on tests because they don't really know how to study for them and need help learning how. That was Lisa's problem. She kept looking and looking at her spelling words but she really needed to spell each one aloud, then write it down, in order to fix the correct spelling in her mind.

When kids like Gerry, who study and seem to know the material, have trouble performing, test trouble can mean one of three things: they have a learning problem that interferes with their ability to get the information from their brains onto paper,

or they need practice in test-taking skills such as reading and following directions, or they suffer from a kind of anxiety that resembles stage fright. Whichever it is, the problem usually gets worse without some help from parents.

Most schools begin using tests (other than spelling tests) in fourth grade, and the emphasis on testing intensifies in middle school. Unfortunately, this focus coincides with a time in their lives when many children are all too ready to think of themselves as stupid, hopeless, or pathetic. A child who doesn't do well on tests may find it hard to go on believing in his or her intelligence when all of the official evidence says otherwise, particularly if the child is only eleven years old!

The learning disabilities factor

Many learning disabilities actually interfere with a child's ability to perform on a test. Ways to compensate depend on what the disability is (see pages 28-31). Some kids, like Gerry, for example, have no problem understanding magnetism or the American Revolution but can't put their knowledge on paper. These kids need to take tests verbally, while others, who can take pen-and-paper tests, may not do well if they must complete the test within a specified time. Fortunately, most schools will allow these children to take untimed tests either at home or in a school's resource room.

What about test anxiety?

Some kids with test anxiety simply fear tests. "It's a kind of performance anxiety," psychologist Dr. David Anderegg explains. "Like a performance, a test is something you have to do *now*. That type of a demand makes some kids tense up—their hearts start to pound, their mouths dry out, and their minds freeze." With each failure, the fear gets worse.

Experts such as Dr. Anderegg believe one way kids get over this fear is by experiences with test success that break the pattern. When students discover that they aren't going to "die" on a test, they're more relaxed and, consequently, can perform better. A sympathetic teacher can create failure-proof tests for your child that ask for opinions and personal experiences and don't depend on right and wrong answers.

Alternatives to traditional tests

Remember, the main reason teachers give tests is to determine whether or not students are learning what they're teaching. There are many ways to do that, and more and more schools today are experimenting with alternatives that are especially suited to kids who are anxious about tests.

One is the take-home exam. At home, if a child begins to feel anxious, he can step away and relax for a few minutes, then continue. Another is a student portfolio. A fifth grader who is studying the ocean, for example, might be graded on a scrapbook on whales that includes a report, photographs, a map of migratory routes, and an exchange of e-mail with a whale researcher from halfway around the world.

How to help kids study for tests

We often forget that how to study for and take tests are skills that can be learned.

First of all, we have to show our kids how to set up a study schedule that avoids last-minute cramming panic. Reviewing math facts for ten minutes each day for a week is more effective than spending forty minutes on Thursday night. Basic study techniques, like breaking information into small chunks in order to memorize it, reviewing by outlining and explaining to someone else, and making sure you focus study efforts on the right things, are all keys to test success.

Lots of practice with old sample tests at home helps children become familiar with test formats and the different kinds of questions on tests, such as multiple choice, as well as master essentials, such as reading and following test directions.

Advising an anxious child, "Just stay calm and do your best," is like advising a child who can't swim to relax when he finds himself in water over his head. Instead, teach relaxation techniques and make up a card with a positive statement — "You're prepared and will do a great job!"— that kids can take with them. ❏

ADVICE FROM KIDS

○ "When I walk into a test, I do meditation and relaxing exercises that athletes do before a game. For 1 minute I think about a special place I love to sit—a couch on my screened porch. Then I breathe in to the count of 4, hold it for 4 beats, breathe out to the count of 4 and hold it for 4 beats. I don't look at the test paper until I'm really feeling calm, and if I begin to feel anxious I just do it again," reports Kate, 12.

About Cheating

- **"Moral standards have become so eroded that many children can no longer tell right from wrong,"** explains Dr. Kevin Ryan, founding director of the Center for the Advancement of Ethics and Character at Boston University. **"Kids no longer have a moral compass other than enlightened self-interest."**

   When schools don't punish kids who are caught cheating, students sometimes interpret this "relaxed" attitude as tacit approval of cheating.

Many parents remember vividly the first time they attempted to cheat on a paper or an exam, usually at some point in middle school. Because elementary schools focus more on cooperative learning than they do on individual accomplishment, young children rarely feel a need to cheat. But when they enter middle school, with exams, honor roll, high honor roll, and sometimes even highest honor roll, the pressure is on, and many kids begin to think about all the possible ways they can be winners—cheating among them.

For me, the temptation was an eighth-grade social studies test. I raced to meet a friend who had just taken the test so that she could tell me what the essay was. When we met, my heart was pounding, and by the time I got to my seat, I was a nervous wreck, ravaged by guilt. My eyes went instantly to the essay. It was different! The truth is, I was relieved! Most of our kids have been or will be tempted to cheat at some point in their school careers, too.

Cheating is very common

Although most research regarding cheating is about high schools, a recent survey conducted in two U.S. schools and nine international schools in Switzerland, Austria, Italy, and Germany showed that cheating is widespread in middle-level schools. Educators agree that middle school is where kids learn to cheat, and the most common forms of it are copying, plagiarism, and crib sheets.

The superintendent of schools in my district admits that the statistics on cheating for middle schoolers are similar to those in a survey of 3,100 top high school juniors and seniors conducted for *Who's Who Among American High School Students.* Seventy-eight percent said they often cheated on exams and eighty-nine percent said cheating was common at their schools. Remarkably, none of the kids seemed to feel guilty or worried about it.

Though cheating is a middle-school issue, the attitudes that lead to it start much earlier. If we want our kids to resist temptation then, we have to foster different attitudes from the time they start school.

Why kids cheat

The main reason for cheating is a practical one—to get good grades. If all we focus on with our children is how good—or bad—their grades are, they grow up thinking that they'd better get good grades no matter what they have to do to get them. In other words, asking our kids a question such as "What are you learning about in social studies?" is better than "What grade did you get on the social studies test?"

Kids also cheat sometimes when they haven't logged enough time studying. We can help our kids set priorities—homework and study, then TV—and remind them of their responsibilities. Do they have an exam coming up? Have they studied? It's important to ask. When kids don't finish their homework or neglect studying and there are no consequences, they stop feeling responsible.

Yet another reason kids give for cheating is that age-old cry, "But everyone else is doing it!"—a justification for all kinds of behavior once kids enter middle school.

Unfortunately, attitudes of "success at any cost" have even penetrated school administrations. In a 1990 national survey of educators, one in eleven teachers reported pressure from administrators to alter standardized test results before reporting scores. To students, this kind of climate is a powerful rationale for cheating, especially if we don't actively teach different values. It's easy to forget that kids learn their most important lessons about personal integrity from us. If a merchant hands you a ten-dollar bill instead of a single while he's giving you change and you keep it, you're teaching your kids about cheating.

If your child does cheat

When one father found out that his eighth-grade son, Ian, received an A on a paper that had actually been written by a friend, he wasn't sure what to do. "I was torn," he admits. "I wanted Ian to know

I disapproved of what he had done, but I didn't want to get him in trouble at school."

That night, however, he overheard his son boasting about what he'd done on the phone, "Naw, I don't really feel guilty because I got such a good grade—and besides, I paid Jay ten dollars to write that paper." That was the impetus his father needed. He told Ian, "I want you to know that our family doesn't approve of cheating. Unless you admit to your teacher that you didn't write this paper, I am going to."

Ian was furious at his dad, started crying, and promised he'd never do it again if his dad did nothing. But his dad held firm. Ian received a failing grade and was very angry at his dad. But experts agree with the way Ian's dad handled the problem. ❏

About Homework Hassles

"**I** know this sounds extreme," admits Don, the father of a third grader and a sixth grader, "but I feel as if David and Emily's homework is ruining my life and our family relationships! Every night we get into fights, and by the time we go to bed, we all feel strung out and angry. The worst part is that my wife, Pat, and I don't know how to extricate ourselves."

Does Don's complaint sound familiar? To many parents it probably does. Homework is one of the hottest areas of concern among parents, even those with children in the first and second grades!

It's not surprising that we're all so anxious—most current research stresses the fact that children whose parents are involved in their schoolwork are much better students and become much more successful adults. On the other hand, experts advise parents to avoid over-involvement and emotional confrontations with their children over homework so it doesn't become a power struggle.

How do we walk this fine line? The key lies in assessing where homework fits into your child's learning and how both fit into your life.

How much homework is typical

Most parents don't realize there's a surprising variation among schools and teachers in how much homework kids have, how homework is used, and how much parents are expected to be involved with it. One of my sons averaged almost two hours a night of homework when he was in second grade. (Most parents and teachers

DID YOU KNOW?

◆ Schools across the country are setting up homework centers and homework hotlines so that when a parent can't help with homework, another available adult can.

◆ A recent study showed that 1/3 of parents had trouble helping with homework because things are being taught so differently today.

would consider this much too long.) His big brother—a ninth grader at the time—had considerably less to do. The next year the situation was reversed.

What this means for parents is that unless your school district has a very clear, consistent homework policy, you'll need to touch base with teachers early each year to avoid a lot of questions and problems. If you find out how much time a teacher expects students to spend on homework each night, you'll know whether your child is spending too much or too little time to complete it. Experts suggest the following: first grade, 15 to 20 minutes; second grade, 25; third grade, 30; fourth grade, 35; fifth grade, 40; sixth grade, 45; seventh grade, 50; and eighth grade, 60.

The purposes of homework

Knowing how teachers use homework helps parents figure out how to help their kids.

Mrs. Vasallo, like many elementary school teachers, assigns homework to reinforce what went on in class. Her assignments are generally review work: read over your notes, look at your spelling test, work on the words you missed, and prepare for a retest. When we help our kids with this kind of review, we find out what's going on in class. And if a child is expected to go over notes, but has no notes to go over, it tells you that something that should be happening isn't!

Mr. Foley takes another tack: he uses homework to prepare students for what's going to be happening in class the next day. When kids are studying immigration, they might be asked to talk to their parents and grandparents about where their family came from. Parents can make this kind of research come alive for kids by providing photographs and shared memories.

Some teachers think of homework as a way of allowing children to practice what goes on in class at their own pace. When teachers use homework this way, parents can let teachers know where they see strengths and weaknesses.

In addition, almost all teachers believe that homework helps children learn to take responsibility for their work.

What's your role?

To help, check over, and correct it? Or not? Many schools don't provide guidelines about this or any other homework issues for parents, so most of us are left wondering what constitutes help and support. Where is the line between helping our children and doing their homework for them? What should we do when our children wail, "If you loved me, you would help me," by which they usually mean "Write my paper for me"? The Parent Tips box on page 69 provides some suggestions.

On whether or not to correct homework, many teachers agree with my son's second-

AGE FACTOR
A HOMEWORK SUPPLIES KIT

❖ **Kindergarten to 3rd grade:** pencils, pens, crayons, markers, erasers, and a pencil sharpener; lined paper and construction paper; tape and glue; ruler and scissors; paper clips and a small stapler; a children's dictionary.

❖ **Fourth grade and up:** Add in file folders to keep papers, cover folders for reports, index cards, and a hole punch. For middle-school kids, a dictionary, an almanac, atlases of the world and the U.S., and a globe should be part of your family's homework library. For Internet resources and a good series of reference books, see pages 95-96.

ASK THE EXPERTS

Homework's hidden agenda:

• "Teachers adore kids who do their homework," says Dr. Mary DeBey, an early childhood educator, "and they adore parents of kids who do their homework. If kids aren't doing well in school but come to class with their homework done, teachers often think they're doing well. And if kids are doing well in school but don't do homework, teachers often think of them as trouble. Doing homework is one of the things that tells teachers that you and your child are supportive of them and their efforts."

grade teacher, who advocated a hands-off homework policy. "If you correct his work," she pointed out to me, "how will I be able to see what he does and doesn't know?" If you agree with this approach, you may be surprised to hear that some teachers don't. The very next year my son complained he was getting low grades on homework because we weren't correcting it. He exclaimed, upset, "It isn't fair! Everyone else's parents correct theirs, and those kids get high grades."

Check with each teacher to find out the ways he or she expects parents to be involved with children's homework.

Getting it done

Most parents think the most difficult issue about the H word, as a friend puts it, is the struggle to see that it gets done. If your children are like most, they fight when you suggest getting down to work, dawdle until bedtime, and then moan about how much they have to do, or they stubbornly assert, "I don't have any homework tonight," or "The teacher says we don't have to do the homework if we know how to do the math problems." I know only one solution to this kind of procrastination: a regular study schedule.

When. There is no right time for homework, but starting at the same time every day is important. Some kids, like my younger son, do best if they sit down right after school, while they're still in a "school mode." Other kids need some time to jump, run, or just be dreamy first and are refreshed and ready to work after dinner. Most parents find that kids are more likely to stick to "homework time" if they get to pick the time. If your child discovers that his choice isn't working well, he can always change it.

Keeping to a specific amount of time, such as thirty minutes or an hour, avoids those claims of "no homework tonight." If the claim is really true, I remind kids this is a study time—they can practice spelling words, review a chapter or math facts, or read a good book.

Where. After many years, I've arrived at one hard and fast rule: homework can NEVER be done in front of the TV. Beyond that, find a comfortable place with good light, space to spread out books, and no distractions. I used to believe that the best place was at a desk in a child's room. My own kids, however, like to sprawl at the kitchen table, especially if my husband or I are there preparing dinner.

Standards. Another big problem for parents is what the homework looks like when it's done. When I was a child, I would no sooner have handed in a wrinkled sheet of homework with chocolate smears on the corner than I would have walked into class naked. Yet my son, who is a first-rate student, thinks nothing of it. "Don't you care about doing a good job?" I entreat. This kind of nagging is futile. Other parents complain that their kids eke out only the minimum. "If the teacher says to write a few sentences," one mom observed, "my daughter will count out exactly three sentences. 'The teacher said only a few,' she'll say, 'and three is a few.'"

Both are issues of pride, but experts agree that harping about sloppiness isn't the answer. Instead, we can let children know when we don't think they've done a very neat or complete job and ask them if they're really satisfied with this kind of work. They may tell us that their teacher doesn't care—which may or may not be accurate. And that may mean that it's time for you to have a talk with the teacher, just to set things straight. ❏

▶ PARENT TIPS

▶ **Giving help and support.** "Support does *not* mean doing children's homework for them. It does mean providing supplies, being willing to drive to the library, holding kids to their responsibilities, teaching them how to be organized and plan ahead, and respecting effort even if the result isn't a perfect job. Taking over encourages dependence and robs them of a sense of accomplishment," advises Mitch, father of 3.

▶ **When kids get emotional about homework.** "Sometimes children wail, 'I can't do this' or 'It's too hard.' Usually this means, 'I'm overwhelmed and don't know where to begin.' Doing a 3-page report may seem like climbing Mt. Everest. First, have them take a break to calm down. Ask them to talk through the assignment. Write down what they say. Then help them divide it into smaller parts. Sometimes just seeing their ideas on paper is enough to get them started," counsels Sharon, mother of 2.

▶ **If you find out your child isn't handing in homework.** "We had Emma sign a contract agreeing to do her homework, and we signed it, too. It specified that when she had no homework, she would spend at least 15 minutes going over notes. We also asked the teacher to call us whenever she failed to hand in a homework so she wouldn't fall behind," reports Eileen, mother of 1.

▶ **Don't expect perfection.** "Remember it's typical for kids to find it hard to get down to homework and want to rush through it. Don't order, nag, threaten, or punish. Admitting that you sometimes don't want to work, either, helps," says Joe, father of 2.

When To Have Your Child Tested

My advice: sooner rather than later. I've never heard any parent who worried about a child's school problems say, "I'm sorry we had her tested." The common story parents tell is this: "I'm sorry we didn't take our child for testing earlier. We could have avoided so much stress and pain for ourselves and our child." Undiagnosed learning disabilities usually cause kids' self-esteem to sink lower and lower and often create social problems, too.

That was the case with Jenny, a third grader, whose parents heard for three years, "Your daughter is so bright, but she just won't try." At first they worried, but after a while, they felt angry at their child. When they finally discovered how extensive Jenny's learning disabilities were, they felt terrible because they'd been blaming her for things that were beyond her control. "Why didn't anyone suggest testing?" they wondered.

The truth is that many teachers don't always recognize when a child should be tested. So parents should be alert to these red flags that signal learning disabilities:

Red Flag #1: Trust your feelings

No one knows a young child as intimately as his or her parents. If you have a gut feeling that something is wrong with the way your child is progressing in school, think of it as a warning—look very closely at what's going on in school and bring up the idea of testing with your child's teacher or the school psychologist.

Red Flag #2: Teachers are puzzled

When teachers often make statements about your child's performance in school such as, "I know Alec is very bright, but he just won't settle down and learn his spelling," or "Zoe is so smart, but she just doesn't

seem to want to learn," or "I know John could do this work if only he would try!" a bell should go off in your head.

Teachers who don't understand why or are frustrated that your child isn't learning may attribute his difficulties to laziness, willfulness, and other assorted dreadful character traits. We all know that kids can be lazy and stubborn, but try to remember that young children almost always start out wanting to learn. In the struggles that consume a child with learning problems, this simple fact often gets lost. Says Jenny's mom, "Finally we asked ourselves, 'Why would Jenny subject herself to so much grief if she could escape it by memorizing a few easy spelling words?'"

Red Flag #3: Early speech problems

When a child's speech doesn't mature at the same rate as that of his peers, it sometimes means he has problems processing language and isn't hearing the same sounds other children his age are hearing. Experts find that these children are much more likely to have language-related learning problems, specifically problems with reading and writing, which don't show up until they begin learning to read and write in school. I'm not suggesting that you have your child tested just because he is slow to talk, but if that problem is coupled with any of the other red flags I've mentioned, it's a good reason to have him evaluated.

Red Flag #4: Your child hates school

First, rule out social problems—a class bully who's tormenting everyone, tight little cliques that your child just can't navigate, and so on. Sometimes, teachers don't yet suspect kids have a learning problem, particularly when children are in kindergarten or first grade, but children themselves have a strong sense that something is askew.

Maybe they realize they're putting in much more effort than the other children and don't seem to be doing as well. Maybe they feel lost, frightened, or different because others seem to catch on when they don't. All these feelings may lead to much unhappiness and a strong dislike of school—even though children themselves don't recognize and can't really explain the reasons behind their feelings.

Red Flag #5: Check family history

Experts agree that learning disabilities run in families. If your child is having trouble at school, think back along your family tree. Was there a sibling, parent, aunt, uncle, who had problems in school? Kids suffered from learning disabilities even before anyone knew what they were. A generation or two ago, children with learning disabilities were regarded as problems, stupid, or "smart, but just not a student." Family history coupled with another red flag is definitely an indication that testing might be in order. ❑

AGE FACTOR

❖ "Every year that a child suffers with undiagnosed learning disabilities makes an impact on how a child perceives himself as a learner. But 1st grade is especially critical because 1st graders are just beginning to compare themselves, as learners, to other kids," explains Wendy Rubin, co-director of Pinnacle Resources, Inc., a nonprofit learning organization in Massachusetts.

If Your Child Is Gifted

My cousin's gifted son, Sean, was studying the Civil War in first grade. At our family Thanksgiving that year we heard about the Blue and the Gray, about what it meant for a nation to fight against itself, about slavery, about Lincoln, and we listened as he recited the Gettysburg Address, by heart, while all the other kids were playing hide and seek. When he was done, we suggested that he go and play, too, but soon he came running back to tell me that my two boys were fighting, and observed, "It's like a Civil War when two brothers fight."

Sean was wonderful, but Sean was also a royal pain. I found him fascinating, and I found him irritating. And it occurred to me later that night that his teachers and classmates probably felt very much the same way about him.

Is your child gifted?

According to Priscilla Vail, author of *Gifted, Precocious, or Just Plain Smart*, gifted children share some—but not necessarily all—of these ten common traits, and a few can cause kids problems in school:

Instant knowledge. They often seem to grasp concepts and ideas almost immediately, without having to work to learn them. As you can imagine, this is highly annoying to peers.

Pleasure in seeing patterns. They see connections in the world that most of us miss. When eight-year-old Tom heard the phone numbers of two of his parents' friends, 932-4907 and 932-5109, he remarked instantly, "Oh! They're the same plus two."

Extreme drive, curiosity, energy, and concentration. The intensity of these four qualities can drive everyone else crazy. In a fifth-grade math class, Bethany got excited about all the other possible ways to solve the same equation and kept going until her teacher and classmates lost patience with her. She came home feeling terribly wounded. She wasn't trying to be difficult—but her need to think of all the possibilities was just as essential to her as her need to eat.

Empathy. If they have a strong sense of self-esteem and feel good about themselves in general, gifted kids use their empathic skills benevolently. But if they feel left out, awkward, and unloved, they know how to make very wounding remarks. This capacity can trigger all kinds of social problems at school and add to a gifted child's sense of isolation.

Memory. Rote memory is not a strong point of gifted kids—in fact, they're often bad at memorizing lists that they find boring, which some teachers find very hard to understand. On the other hand, they'll surprise you with their recall of what's important to them, like how many traps the lobsterman pulled in the morning you accompanied him last summer.

Heightened perception. Joy and sorrow, beauty and ugliness . . . gifted children see and feel things in a more intense way than most of us, and sometimes this makes it difficult for them to be satisfied with their own work. "I'm never painting again," a child may say when the efforts of his hands don't match the picture in his mind. Lots of encouragement is called for from teachers and parents when these situations arise!

Divergent thinking. These kids love questions and ideas and coming up with different answers for the same questions. A child who loves to think about "What if . . ." will have a hard time with a teacher who wants a "yes" or a "no" answer written neatly on a page in a workbook.

Treat gifted kids like children

Teachers often expect children who are intellectually precocious to be more mature and organized than others their age. But when it comes to emotional and social development, they can be behind. The fact that Sean had an extraordinary grasp on the Civil War didn't prevent him from having a tantrum because all the brownies contained nuts! It helps to remind teachers that gifted kids can be just as childish as other kids.

Don't overschedule

In an effort to make sure they are encouraging their kids' interests and providing sufficient challenges, parents of gifted children sometimes make the mistake of piling on too many activities. Janie's dad, for example, insisted that she take piano, gymnastics, and a special Saturday math class for gifted kids at the local college. She had no time for pajama parties, freeze tag, or, most important, just hanging out with other kids her age—no wonder she felt left out and different at school!

Ways to get the school's cooperation

Look hard for ways in which your child's teachers excel and send notes thanking them, as Carol's parents did with her science teacher. His fascinating experiments really excited Carol's interest—and the more her parents thanked him, the harder he worked to challenge her. Don't approach any teacher about what you can do together to meet your child's needs until after you've laid a solid groundwork of appreciation.

Ask teachers to keep you informed about your child's emotional well-being. Gifted kids need to know that they can sometimes fail and still be valued. Though Carol was a superstar academically and tutored many of her classmates in math and English, she was also the only kid in the class who couldn't climb the rope in gym. Fortunately, her parents and teachers saw this as an opportunity for Carol's friends to help her out, and everyone came out a winner. ❏

ADVICE FROM KIDS

Here are a few common complaints from gifted kids:

○ "Kids tease us about being brains," says Al, 11.

○ "Sometimes being good at many things is confusing," adds Tanya, 8.

○ "Everyone expects us to always do the best we can. We aren't perfect!" protests April, 10.

○ "It's hard to find friends who can really understand what we feel and talk about what we're interested in," reports Matt, 13.

○ "School is boring and too easy," says Sara, 7.

○ "We always feel different," complains Allie, 12.

Skipping A Grade & Staying Back

On my last day of second grade, I ran home eager to show Mom my all As report card and puzzled about the message "You have been promoted to class 4-A" on the back. All my friends had been promoted to 3-A or 3-B. What did it mean? When my mom called the school to find out, she learned that I was one of four second graders who had skipped third grade.

Fortunately, this isn't how parents today find out a school wants a child to skip or repeat a grade. But the reasons why and the problems it can cause haven't changed.

What's the rationale?

Both retention (staying in the same grade for another year) and skipping a grade are motivated by the same positive idea: to give children the very best opportunity to learn. If kids are academically advanced enough to succeed in classes beyond the ones traditional for their age, so the rationale goes, they should be allowed to. Students who are struggling to keep pace, on the other hand, should be placed where they can catch up. On a theoretical level this makes sense. But in reality, academic issues are only part of a child's school life.

The biggest problem

As you might guess, the social consequences of taking students away from their peer group and placing them with younger or older children can have a profound impact—a fact I learned the hard way. I went into fourth grade without having learned to write in cursive or to divide. And I left many of my good friends behind. I was the smallest in my second grade and seemed even smaller in that fourth grade. All year I struggled to find a place for myself socially and academically.

The latest research: skipping a grade

Research from the National Association for Gifted Children (NAGC) indicates that when gifted children aren't adequately challenged, they simply don't thrive and that skipping is one viable way to offer the educational opportunities and resources they need. But along with others who advocate skipping, NAGC stresses that for it to be successful, the decision must take into consideration a student's emotional readiness as well as his intellectual abilities.

The latest research: retention

Research on the effectiveness of repeating a grade is overwhelmingly negative—yet many teachers still believe it's the only solution for kids having academic trouble. Study after study shows that students who are held back—even those in prefirst-grade programs—continue to have the same academic problems. Retention, invariably, damages self-esteem, and it's particularly damaging for kids with learning disabilities.

How to decide

When Susan's teacher suggested she repeat second grade, her parents said they wanted a complete evaluation of Susan before a decision was made. They followed the approach that's also used when a child's school recommends skipping. Susan's first- and second-grade teachers, the principal, and the school psychologist met with Susan's parents to talk about Susan's social maturity, friendships, and physical maturity, and get their input on how they—and Susan—felt about her staying back. Any school testing should be shared with you

and explained so that you understand it. Don't be intimidated by edu-babble!

Since Susan's parents were aware that retention rarely solves some academic problems, they asked about alternatives, such as multi-age classes, which are much more effective. Could they help Susan themselves? Schools that educate parents to help their children have better results than schools that practice retention.

If the school recommends skipping, be sure to discuss the idea with your child and to think about long-range consequences. An eight-year-old may have no problem with the academic demands of a fourth-grade class, but will he or she be ready for the organizational ones? What about several years ahead? Boys who love sports can have a very hard time if they're smaller than their classmates.

The best chance for success

Whether your child is retained or skipped, he'll need help to succeed. Make sure the school has a plan for your child when the school year begins. Kids who skip often find it hard to adjust without academic help to bridge the gap between what they missed but need to know, and their parents need to be particularly attentive to helping them keep track of everything. The ability to organize a notebook, maintain an assignment book, and cope with long-range projects requires maturity—and gifted kids aren't necessarily more mature. ❑

Getting The Most From A Parent-Teacher Conference

At least twice a year most parents of school-age kids find themselves waiting outside their child's classroom door for a conference with the teacher. Often we're wondering just what we should expect to hear in our twenty minutes or so of allotted time and what kind of questions we should ask. What we really want to know, after all, is whether our kids are happy, whether they're learning well, and most of all, whether the teacher likes and appreciates them the way we do. If we listen hard during the conference, we'll come away with the answers.

The main purpose of parent-teacher conferences, though, is so the teacher can tell you, in a general way, about what's going on in your child's classroom and, in a more specific way, how your child is doing. They also provide a good opportunity for you to size up the teacher and to share information about your child that can make his or her time in the classroom happier and more productive, and head off problems before they start.

Come prepared with questions

Over the years, Chrissy's mom has learned to spend some time jotting down her concerns before the conference, and she brings them with her, along with the most recent report card. She also checks with her daughter to see whether she has anything she wants her parents to bring up—she knows that Chrissy, like many kids, isn't always comfortable mentioning certain kinds of problems to the teacher.

Has anything significant happened in your child's life recently, such as a death in the family, a new pet, a new sibling? Put that on your list of things to discuss, too. Problems at home may affect your child's behavior at school, and if teachers know, they're better able to help.

Let the teacher know what's important to you

Teachers usually discuss your child's academic achievements, behavior, and relationships with other kids, but be prepared to ask for other information if you want it, as my husband and I did at a conference with my son's first-grade teacher. We sat on pint-size chairs across from her while she informed

► PARENT TIPS

► "At the beginning of school I send my child's teacher a note giving him or her a thumbnail sketch of what my child is like—mentioning particularly any personality traits that are germane to classroom behavior," offers Melanie, mother of 3.

► "I always let the teacher know how much I value her input and tell her that if something is going on in school that involves my child, I want her to call me about it," reports Sally, mother of 2.

us, "Noah's well ahead of most of his class-mates in math concepts and he's starting to write in sentences," and pulled sheet after sheet of work he'd done in class from a folder to show us.

But at this point in Noah's life we had many other concerns, too, and we were glad when she gave us a chance to ask: "Does he have friends? Does he play with girls and boys, or just boys? Does he spend much time alone? Does he build with blocks or prefer games?"

Of course, now that our son is older, our interests are more academically oriented. We ask what they're studying in social studies, how the teacher grades work, about the quality of Noah's written reports, whether he seems to be trying as hard as he can, and how involved he is in class discussion. We want to hear the teacher's assessment of his strengths, where we can help him improve, and some ideas on how to do that.

But throughout it all, I'm also listening to how the teacher talks about him. Do her personality and teaching style fit with his? Does she talk about him with enthusiasm or annoyance? Does she seem to like him—or not?

Handling sensitive issues

Chrissy's mom felt her daughter's teacher assigned too much homework for the fourth grade, but she wasn't sure exactly what to say. In the end, instead of complaining, she asked carefully, "Chrissy is spending two hours a night on homework. Is that what you're expecting?"

Experts agree that this is the right kind of approach whenever you have a sensitive issue to bring up with a teacher—whether it concerns the way he or she teaches reading, handles the problem of unfinished work, or disciplines your child for talking in line. Personal attacks and accusations never pull the teacher to our point of view. If you're not satisfied at the end of the conference, approach the principal.

When there are problems

Of course, you don't have to wait for a scheduled conference. If your child is having trouble with schoolwork or behavior, set up a conference time as soon as you can, so you can figure out what's causing the problem and map out a plan with the teacher to resolve it. Try to see the teacher as your ally rather than an adversary.

Following up

We all like to be appreciated, and teachers are no exception. Following up the conference with a note is one way I've found to begin building a good relationship with

ASK THE EXPERTS

A 5th-grade teacher advises:

• **Don't come late to a conference and don't use up more than your allotted time. If you need more time, ask for another conference.**
• **Listen to what we have to say first. Then ask questions. Bring along paper so you can take notes.**
• **Ask about how we evaluate your child's work, what grades are based on, and for ideas about helping your child at home.**
• **Afterwards, think about what a teacher has said when you're with your child.**
• **Talk to your child about your conference in a way that will be productive.**

a child's teacher. I try to think of one really good point she made during the conference and thank her for taking the time and trouble to think of it. You may be surprised by how much goodwill this engenders for both you and your child.

Sometimes I've come away from a conference knowing that my child is spending his days in an exciting place with someone who understands and likes him. When I don't, I worry, and try to think of how I can help him cope. ❏

Kids don't do well with chaos. They also don't do well with a structure so rigid that there is no room for their own quirks, personalities, and preferences. The challenge we face as parents is to create an environment in our homes somewhere between the two that supports learning and schoolwork so we can prevent some school troubles from developing.

Lest you think this is an easy task, think again. A specific routine or rule that works for one family doesn't always work for another. And what helps one child might be counterproductive for a brother or sister.

Most parents find that a predictable daily framework benefits all the kids in their family. Just like adults, they usually work better when they feel organized and on top of things instead of confused. An added benefit is that settled rules and routines eliminate the on-the-spot decisions and arguments that wear parents—and kids—down. When our kids whine, "Can't I stay up just a little later?" it's easier to respond, "I know you want to, but the rule is eight o'clock bedtime on school nights," than find ourselves in an argument.

Get organized the night before

Being prepared for the next day before going to bed gives parents and kids alike a settled feeling. For one thing, it's more relaxing for kids to go to sleep knowing that they've taken care of business. For another, it makes mornings more pleasant. Here's the routine that works for us:

What my kids do. They check assignment sheets to make sure they haven't forgotten anything, then pack their schoolbags and leave them by the back door. When they were younger, I packed their lunches and left them bagged in the fridge. Now they do. They choose what to wear the next day and lay it out on a chair.

What we do together. We take a look at the calendar for the coming day, which reminds us of any appointments, lessons, long-term assignments that are due, sports practices, after-school activities, or field trips, so we can gather equipment or make driving plans. A paste-it note placed on the front door the night before is a great way to remember to bring in your oboe or permission slips.

We also listen to the weather report. If it's going to be raining, we get out umbrellas and slickers. If it's going to be cold, we dig out the mittens.

What we do at bedtime. Everything goes more smoothly in my house, as in most, when we keep to a regular bedtime routine on school nights. The time and routine will differ depending on the family and children's ages; regularity is the important thing. When children are little, the routine might include reading a story, hearing a special lullaby, and turning on a night light. Older kids might choose to read

Rules & Routines At Home That Help Kids At School

AGE FACTOR

What are appropriate bedtimes? Many parents say:

❖ Kindergarten & 1st grade: 8:00 PM

❖ 2nd & 3rd grade: 8:30 PM

❖ 4th & 5th grade: 9:00 PM

❖ 6th & 7th grade: 9:30 PM

❖ 8th grade: 10:00 PM

in bed on their own for a half-hour. Some children, like mine, take showers; others, especially older ones, prefer to bathe in the morning. But if that means four people will be competing for one shower, work out a rotation in advance that's fair for everyone.

Make mornings pleasant

We all want our children to go to school rested, awake, enthusiastic about and equipped for their day, and eager to learn. The more you've done the night before, the less there is to think about in the morning. And if your family is anything like mine, mornings can be very chaotic and not a great time for thinking.

Getting up. After many experiences of yelling up the stairs for children to wake up, we gave each of our boys an alarm clock. You'll find, as we did, that the sooner kids get used to being responsible for getting themselves up in the morning, the better your morning will be. Some parents start this in third grade; others wait as late as fifth. If your children like to lie in bed awhile, a simple solution is setting alarm clocks a half-hour ahead.

Allot enough time. Cramming down a piece of toast on the way out the door to the bus is not a great way to start the day. Not all kids like a big breakfast, but they're liable to eat more if they have time to dawdle a little. Many busy parents also try to have enough time in the morning for a pleasurable activity with their children—a game of chess, cards, a read-aloud chapter, or just a talk. This is especially helpful to younger kids who are feeling reluctant about leaving their parents.

Create a calm atmosphere. Margaret, the mother of two, always plays CDs of classical music while she and her family are having breakfast. "I read somewhere that children who listen to Mozart while they're studying do better on tests," she says. "I don't know if it's true, but in the morning it sure beats television." In fact, many parents ban morning television watching.

After-school organization

Even if your child takes a break before beginning homework, it's a good idea to establish certain habits the minute he or she walks through the door. Always putting your backpack and papers in the same place—your room, on the table, or on a hook—avoids those "I-can't-find-it" wails when kids are ready to work. Older children need to check their assignment books to remind themselves what their workload is for the day and whether they have any long-term assignments to start on (see pages 66-69).

Keep a family calendar

All parents know how hard it is to keep track of schedules for more than one person. Many families, like the Harrisons, post a month-by-month calendar in the kitchen or family room along with school and team announcements to help them keep track of where every child has to be and when.

The Harrisons, who have three children, use a different color marker for each family member. Music lessons, soccer games, a big report on monkeys due in three weeks—all of it should go on the calendar, and everyone should check it regularly. The Harrisons gather everyone together on Sunday evening to talk about what the week ahead holds. ❏

▶ PARENT TIPS

Seven TV rules that work for different families:

▶ We allow our kids to watch 8 hours of television per week; they get to be in control of what and when they watch.

▶ In our house, we review the *TV Guide* with our child on Sunday night and make a list of the specific programs he chooses for the following week.

▶ One night a week is the designated TV night. On the other nights, the kids have to amuse themselves in other ways.

▶ No one can watch TV until all homework is completed.

▶ To us, watching television is like playing video and computer games. We link the three and establish a limit on the amount of screen time permissible each day.

▶ We told our children that they can watch as much television as they want each day, as long as they spend an equivalent time reading.

▶ Homework can never be done in front of the TV.

Plan Ahead

No one will be surprised to hear that when it comes to school, anticipating problems and planning your way around them are the best ways to prevent them. That's why our family always returns from our summer vacation at least a week and a half before school starts. Then we have time to be prepared for school—buy new clothes, make sure we're set for the first day, and wind down from the free-form pleasures of the summer. But other kinds of planning ahead help, too.

What's hard for your child?

Think about what your child is like and what this year's problems are liable to be. Shy Amanda, for example, usually spends the first few weeks of school unhappily hovering on the edges of activities. This year her mom is determined to figure out how to change that. Mark, on the other hand, is highly competitive and had difficulty last year being less than number one in sports and schoolwork. His parents want this year to be better.

Late August preparation

Many kids, especially those who are disorganized, have trouble going from summer to school mode. That's why Pam, the mother of three, instituted a pre-Labor Day school "prep" day. Even though she doesn't know specifically what supplies her children will need, they all start out at a stationery store. Her aim is simply to get her kids thinking about school by asking questions like "What kind of pencils do you prefer for writing?" or "What color binder do you want this year?"

Each child chooses notebooks, pencils, pens, packs of paper, and whatever else says "School's coming!" to them. Later that day they arrange the supplies on their desks, organize bulletin boards, and get out and pack their backpacks.

A sneak preview

Some kids are like Annabel. Being familiar in advance with the actual classroom and her teacher's face are important to her, so her family always plans a visit to the school the week before it starts. Some kids feel the same kind of anxiety about what they'll be learning. If you have such a child, visit the school yourself before classes begin and ask the teacher for copies of the books your child will be using. Sitting quietly in the safety of home and leafing through these books with your child before school starts can ease his worries. This is particularly helpful for children with learning problems.

Specific subjects

If you know that your child has trouble with a specific subject, like math or reading, try to plan activities over the summer that are related to it. Reading a chapter of a book aloud every evening or joining a library program that rewards children for each book read with stars may keep a reluctant reader reading. One dad reviewed the year's math with his son by planning a short, interesting math activity each week.

At a minimum, meet with the teacher before school starts to let her know what subjects your child has a hard time with. George's mom, for example, asks his new teacher to call her if George is beginning to fall behind in math. This kind of communication not only helps the teacher, but also reinforces the idea that you're working together as a team.

Easing social tension

It's not unusual for kids to fall out of their social swirl during the summer. Often they worry about whether or not they'll still have the same friends when they return to school. "Who'll be in my class?" they ask, anxiously. If your child worries a great deal about social dynamics, call the school for a class list and invite some of the classmates over—one at a time—before school starts.

Setting their inner clock

My children have no bedtime during the summer. They stay up until they're ready to collapse into their beds, and sleep until they're ready to start again. Generally, the natural circadian rhythm that they fall into is quite different from the one their school

schedule demands. Sleep patterns take time to readjust, so I begin easing them into their school clock about two weeks before school starts. Know what your child's sleep needs are—and get things in order before the school year begins.

When your child is sick

The beginning of the school year isn't the only time to plan ahead. Any time our children are out of school for a few days or more can create problems for them if we don't anticipate. Getting assignments from teachers, picking up books from school so our kids can at least glance at what's being covered while they're out, and working with them for an hour or so a day if they're not too sick can prevent them from being far behind when they go back. ❏

How To Be Involved In Your Child's School

Parents usually volunteer in their child's school because they want to help out an overworked teacher or raise money for some special program or activity that will benefit their children. But it turns out that their presence at school has a much more far-reaching impact. Study after study reveals that the children who are the highest academic achievers are the ones whose parents are involved, in some way, in their child's school. These children get a message from their parents that school really matters—that it's worth working for—and that's a powerful reason for us to help in our child's school whatever way we can.

Before you rush in, though, think honestly about how much time you have, where your talents lie, and only then look for the right niche. Even if you work full-time and are on a tight schedule, there will be something you can do.

In your child's class

Volunteering in your child's classroom gives you a valuable opportunity to observe what's going on there, what your child's teacher is like, and how your child interacts with the teacher and other kids. For one thing, if you don't like what you see, you can begin doing something about it. If your child is young, he'll probably be terribly proud and extra industrious when you're there, as Jeff was. When his dad, who had Tuesdays off, spent an hour each week working with math groups, his son's behavior and math enthusiasm improved.

Middle-school kids, on the other hand, often find our very existence mortifying—let alone our presence on their turf. Check first to see how they'll feel if you volunteer—they may eventually agree (even if reluctantly) as my son did when my husband, a writer, spent eight mornings in his seventh-grade class working with students on writing screenplays.

But if you have more limited time, make other arrangements. One working mom takes a personal day once a year so she can talk to her daughter's class about her work. Another makes a point to help set up and chaperone at least one class trip every year.

▶ PARENT TIPS

If You Don't Have Much Time
In families where both parents work outside the home (which is most American families), it can be very difficult to find time to volunteer in your child's school. These busy parents found some ways:

▶ "I write letters to legislators protesting any cuts in educational budgets—and let my kids read the letters," explains Thea, mother of 2.

▶ "I volunteer to be part of a classroom phone chain. It hardly takes any time but helps me feel connected to other parents," says Ted, father of 3.

▶ "I ask the teacher and principal if there's anything I can do to help the school from home in the evenings," reports Marie, mother of 2.

One of my friends enjoys being the "class parent" because she gets to know all the other kids' parents through talking on the phone with them regularly.

Shelving books in the library, helping in the school office, or making costumes for an all-school play are other ways to participate—and it's especially important during times like these, when many schools are facing severe budget cuts.

PTAs and other parent groups

Parent-Teacher Associations and Organizations (PTAs and PTOs) are groups of parents who work together, with teachers as partners or advisers, in a wide range of activities aimed at improving schools.

The elementary-school PTA in our town, for example, initiated and staffed a six-week after-school program in the elementary school that included classes in chess, drama, journalism, toy-making, baking, and carpentry. Our middle-school PTA initiated our first science fair, and one mother, with a special interest in the arts, wrote a grant proposal to bring a nationally renowned poet into the school for an artist-in-residence program.

PTAs have raised money for computers, sponsored speakers on all kinds of important educational issues (including study skills, math, writing, and homework), helped set things in motion to improve communication between teachers, parents, and administrations, and created significant changes for the better in the school's atmosphere. When a middle-school PTA in New York State felt upset with the level of bullying and meanness among students, they hired a speaker to talk about the problem and suggest ways to change it.

Join the school board

There comes a time, usually after one of our children has a very unstimulating year at school, when many of us wish we could make an even bigger impact on school policies and academic expectations and standards. That's what happened to me. One way to do that is be elected to the school board. If you run, though, be prepared for a real commitment of time and energy. I've found that being on the board requires at least twelve hours of work a month—sometimes more—and it can be very frustrating because schools change very slowly. They have a great investment in maintaining the status quo. But I've never regretted my involvement.

During my tenure we've changed many things by hiring new principals for the elementary school and high school, instituting district-wide testing to get a sense of our strengths and weaknesses, and initiating a process of strategic planning that brings the entire community together to talk about what our educational priorities are and how we can make them real. ❑

Does Your Child Need Professional Help?

When our kids are in great shape at school we feel wonderful. When they're having trouble, we feel awful because it hurts to see the children we love suffering.

Despite the nostalgia about childhood, most parents know that for children ages five to thirteen, school isn't always a bed of roses. All kids go through rough times. They hate their friends, flunk tests, talk back to a teacher, don't hand in homework, and more. Usually, we can help them with these school difficulties through changes at home and with the teacher's assistance, and find some calm before the next storm.

When our efforts aren't enough

Sometimes, though, our children get stuck in a rough time. If so, experts advise parents to ask themselves some questions.

First, is it an emergency situation? Few of us would hesitate to seek professional help if a child were setting fires at school or was so terrified of going to school that he had nightmares about it. Think about whether the problem is a chronic one and what might have triggered it. When did it start? How long has it been going on? Did it coincide with any changes at home or school? Is your child having continuing difficulties with other kids at school or ongoing struggles with learning that affect other parts of his life?

When two or three spheres of a child's life (home, school, and peer relationships) are difficult, and when they've been difficult for more than just a short time, you would be wise to get some professional help, the way Carrie's mom did. Nine-year-old Carrie had been an excellent student the previous year, but now, midway through fourth grade, is failing three subjects, is convinced she has no friends, and has frequent angry fights with her parents.

What kind of help?

If the problem is about learning, start with your pediatrician and move on to a neuropsychologist for testing (see pages 32-34 and 70-71). If the problem is emotional, your pediatrician may refer you to a psychiatrist, psychologist, or social worker. The most important factor—more so than the academic degree—is whether a person is state-licensed and has special training and experience in working with children.

What to tell kids

Give your child some idea of who you'll see, what will happen, and why you're going. One dad told his son the psychologist they were going to see was a "worry doctor." Though his son claimed, "I'm not worried," his mom and dad told him they were worried because he didn't want to go to school, didn't seem to have his old friends anymore, and that they wanted to help figure out how to make school—and everything else—fun for him again. ❏

YEAR BY YEAR

What To Expect At Different Ages

What Do Schools Expect From Kids At Different Ages?

We all know that schools have academic goals for each grade, but many parents aren't as aware of teachers' expectations for our children's social and emotional development. If our children don't meet those expectations when others do, they're liable to have trouble at school—even if they are academically smart. Knowing what teachers expect helps parents figure out whether their child is going to need some extra help to prevent or ease trouble at school.

Kindergarten: getting in step

● *Emerging independence.* For some kids, kindergarten marks the first big separation from their family. They have to be able to cope with the events of any given day—both disappointments and triumphs—on their own, put the urge to see Mom or Dad or a familiar babysitter on hold, become more self-reliant, and learn to turn to adults other than parents for help.

● *Learning to be part of a group.* Sitting in a circle, standing in a line, and working with other kids to build a block town are part of a typical kindergarten day. These activities are not as easy for kids as they seem to us—they require that kids have many social skills, such as being able to compromise and to control the impulse to shout or jump up when they feel like it.

● *Staying on task.* In preschool, kids can start coloring a picture and move on to building with blocks when their interest wanes. But in kindergarten they begin learning to stay with a task, working until it's finished. Very short, focused activities like tracing a sheet of numbers or telling a story are designed to help kids do that.

First Grade: getting serious

● *Stronger task focus.* Being able to complete a task is even more important than it was in kindergarten because in most schools first grade is the year most kids learn to read and understand numbers. This requires an ability to focus on serious work that may not always be fun. Even smart kids may fall behind if they can't focus this way or have trouble with frustration.

● *Responding to authority.* First graders are expected to listen when it's required, wait their turn, and do what the teacher asks. The atmosphere in kindergarten is more lenient. But first-grade teachers have much more academic work to cover. For kids that means more sitting down, more listening, and more self-control are necessary. Some kids find all this very difficult.

● *Seeing their place in the world.* First graders are beginning to see themselves and their families in a wider context and recognize differences and similarities. They often find a passionate "best" friend who is "just like" them. Bear in mind that these intense friendships may last anywhere from an hour to a year!

Second Grade: learning to think

● **Becoming more abstract and conceptual.** Second graders are just beginning to think in an abstract way. Rather than manipulating objects in order to do math—like counting marbles—they can now usually think about numbers in their heads.

● **Problem solving.** Most schools expect second graders to start using problem-solving skills—being able to think about a problem, come up with possible solutions, evaluate them, and choose one to try. Teachers assume children will use these skills in both academic work like math and in dealing with other kids. Those who are good at problem solving usually get along much better in school.

Third & Fourth Grade: doing a good job

● **Academic polish.** By now it's no longer enough for your children just to complete a task; how good a job they've done is also important. Teachers want to see work that's neatly written, math that's been checked for errors, and well-organized and well-presented reports.

● **Planning ahead.** Children start learning to keep track of long-range assignments in fourth and late third grade. A spelling test every Friday means doing a bit of studying each night. A report due in two weeks means mapping out a step-by-step plan. As most parents learn, this ability doesn't come as naturally to our kids as procrastination seems to. Often we don't recognize how much they need our help in developing thinking-ahead strategies.

● **Developing camaraderie.** Children begin to have a strong sense of themselves vis-à-vis the group, as in "I'm a sports kind of kid, and so are my friends." Trouble may arise if your child has no interests in common with his classmates.

Fifth & Sixth Grade: the importance of peers

● **Peer pressure.** At this age children have a great need to conform, so peer pressure can have a big impact on school performance, both positive and negative. Many are so distracted by social issues that academic responsibilities take a back seat or get lost in the shuffle.

● **Changeable moods.** Typically students are happy one day, miserable the next, love school one day, hate it the day after. A best friend changes to a worst enemy overnight. All this moodiness takes a toll on life in school just as it does on family life at home, and some kids are moodier than others. Many teachers rely on a fairly structured class environment to counterbalance kids' internal chaos, with spelling tests every Friday, homework every Tuesday and Thursday, and so on.

● **Study skills.** Being able to study effectively for tests, apportion study time appropriately, and keep track of long-range

ASK THE EXPERTS

• "Our understanding of development has a good side and a bad side," says Dr. Susan Engel, a professor of developmental psychology at Bennington College. "The good side is that most schools recognize that 4-year-olds and 8-year-olds are quite different and have different ways of learning. The bad side is that many people think of development as a rigid timetable. If kids don't appear at the right station at the right time, alarms go off. Development is not a smooth, even ride—kids develop at different rates. And sometimes they go through slumps. That doesn't always mean there's a problem."

assignments are now highly important. Can students always do it? Of course not.

• *Being organized.* In most schools these grades mark the beginning of departmentalization. Students now move around from classroom to classroom and have more than one teacher. Many kids react to this shift, as mine did, by becoming even more disorganized and distracted than they were before: forgotten homework, lunches, jackets, shoes (yes, shoes!), and panic about tests that they forgot to study for are extremely common.

Seventh & Eighth Grade: growing up

• *Developing self-motivation and an identity.* Some of the emotional and organizational turmoil of the last two years begins to ease, to parents' relief. Seventh graders now look for their own niche in music, sports, theater, and art. If they find an area of interest, they usually apply themselves with surprising energy, and this self-motivation spills over into schoolwork.

• *Sex, sex, sex.* Well, not really, but both boys and girls are beginning to think about IT, and that can be very consuming. What adds to social difficulties are physical differences. No other grade has a wider range of physical development than seventh grade. There are boys who look like fourth graders and boys who need to shave. There are girls with breasts and girls who haven't begun to develop yet.

Signs of Learning Disabilities—By Age

The symptoms of learning disabilities are age-related. Remember: a child can show some of them but not actually have a disability—he or she may just be slow in developing a particular skill.

• *First Grade: using language.* Difficulty learning to read, reversing letters and shapes, not distinguishing short vowel sounds or syllables in a word, and omitting endings and punctuation are signs of disabilities, as is difficulty using a pencil. Non-academic problems include allergies, many nightmares and tantrums, and problems following directions at school and at home.

• *Second & third grade: expressing ideas.* The symptoms common to first graders persist into second and third grade. But teachers also note that these kids have increasing difficulty expressing their ideas in words or on paper and are more likely to complain about frequent headaches.

• *Fourth grade & up: low self-esteem.* Two types of symptoms are common among middle schoolers who have undiagnosed learning disabilities, and both reflect low self-esteem. One is academic—reluctance to read, write, and do any schoolwork. The other is behavioral—getting into fights, withdrawing socially, having a negative attitude toward school and life, and being anxious, depressed, or easily frustrated. ❑

WE RECOMMEND
Books, The Internet, & CD-ROM

BOOKS

For Kids in Elementary School

ARTHUR'S TEACHER TROUBLE
by Marc Brown (Little, Brown, 1987)

This year lovable Arthur has the strictest teacher in the school. He's sure that third grade will be trouble. Great illustrations combined with an appealing plot make this a winner for younger kids.

AMBER BROWN IS NOT A CRAYON
by Paula Danziger (Scholastic 1994)

A fun book for early readers about a great friendship torn asunder. Now who's going to help Amber with her fractions?

AMBER BROWN GOES FOURTH
by Paula Danziger (Scholastic, 1994)

Another winner in this series. This time Amber is gathering what she needs to begin fourth grade. New notebooks, sneakers, pencils, and . . . a really best friend. How do you get one of those?

THE BEAST IN MS. ROONEY'S ROOM
by Patricia Reilly Giff (Dell, 1984)

Richard "Beast" Best has been left back, so for him September means the same old teacher, same old work, and lots of terrible teasing. But somehow, he begins to shine, and the same old stuff takes on new glitter.

SHARK IN SCHOOL
by Patricia Reilly Giff (Yearling, 1994)

Matthew Jackson is starting over in a new school where, he hears, everyone is really mean. In fact, his teacher's nickname is "shark." Matthew's scared and a terrible reader, but things take an unexpected turn for the better by the end of this book.

MATH CURSE
by Jon Scieszka + Lane Smith (Viking, 1995)

A beautiful and very funny picture book for all ages that begins with Mrs. Fibonacci saying, "You know, you can think of almost everything as a math problem." The curse is that you just can't stop! For example, if mail + box = mailbox, does tunafish + tunafish = fournafish? For ages >6 and <99.

THE FLUNKING OF JOSHUA T. BATES
by Susan Shreve (Bullseye Books, 1995)

Why would the smartest kid in third grade need to repeat a year? His teachers say that Joshua T. Bates needs time to "mature." It's pure torture until things start to click and Joshua finds his place . . . where he really does belong.

OLIVER PIG AT SCHOOL
by Jean Van Leeuwen, pictures by Ann Schweninger (Puffin Books, 1994)

Oliver Pig is a nervous wreck about starting kindergarten, but once he meets his grandmotherly teacher it's smooth sailing all the way.

BROWN PAPER SCHOOL SERIES
(Little, Brown 1975)

This series of lively books filled with puzzles, games, and great learning experiences was written by a group of California teachers, writers, and artists. Many will appeal to fifth and sixth graders, too. Titles include: *The I Hate Mathematics! Book* (1975), *The Book of Think* (1976), *The Reasons for the Seasons* (1975), and *Math for Smarty Pants: Or, Who Says Mathematicians Have Little Pig Eyes?* (1982).

For Kids in Middle School

ADAM ZIGZAG
by Barbara Barrie
(Laurel Leaf Books, 1996)

Adam is rich, popular, and handsome. He's also so severely dyslexic and so desperate that he's ready to try anything . . . drugs included. He and his family struggle to find the right school. All ends well, but much happens before the happy ending.

ALL KINDS OF MINDS:
A Young Student's Book about Learning Abilities and Learning Disorders
by Dr. Mel Levine
(Educators Publishing Service, 1993)

A renowned pediatrician and learning-disability specialist, Levine has written a wonderful, funny, and touching book for kids to read by themselves (or for grownups to read to kids) about what school is like for kids who learn "differently." First rate!

SIDEWAYS ARITHMETIC FROM WAYSIDE SCHOOL
by Louis Sachar (Scholastic, 1992)

This collection of fifty hilarious math puzzles that require only simple math skills to solve are taken from Mrs. Jewls's math class at strange and wonderful Wayside School. Look for the second volume, too!

THERE'S A BOY IN THE GIRL'S BATHROOM
by Louis Sachar
(Random House, 1987)

He might be the weirdest kid in school, but he's not totally hopeless—especially once he has the help of a truly compassionate school counselor. A great tale of triumph for any kid who has ever felt like, or worried about becoming, the underdog . . . and that means every kid!

HELP! MY TEACHER HATES ME:
A School Survival Guide for Kids 10-14 Years Old
by Meg Schneider (Workman, 1994)

Kids, whether they're having trouble or not, will find this kid-friendly compendium of advice very useful. It offers a sensitive but no-nonsense approach to a wide variety of school-related problems, including peer pressure, homework, cheating, and more.

BAD GIRLS
by Cynthia Voigt (Scholastic, 1997)

This Newbery-award winning author has created a contemporary story of two fifth-grade girls, Margalo and Mikey, who manage to act out in school at every opportunity. Their experiences and thoughts reveal the complicated emotions that affect the way kids socialize at school at this age.

For All Kids
BRAIN QUEST SERIES
(Workman Publishers)

Lots of question-and-answer cards packed in plastic containers and organized by age, grade, and subject are fun for car trips or the half-hour after dinner and educational, too. Now the series also includes card games. Subjects include: math, American history, logic, science, and English, and the range is all the way from first grade through seventh.

For Parents
HELP ME TO HELP MY CHILD:
A Sourcebook for Parents of Learning Disabled Children
by Jill Bloom (Little, Brown, 1991)

This book stands out from the rest because Bloom, herself the mother of a learning-disabled child, really understands the frustration of both kids and parents in dealing with the educational establishment. A valuable sourcebook that brings together the vast array of information you need in order to take charge and get your kids the help they need.

PARENTING A TO Z:
Mom and Dad's Guide to Everything from Conception to College
by David Brownstone and Irene Franck (HarperCollins, 1996)

Although this book is not specifically about schools or problems with school, it's an absolutely essential reference that manages to include much needed school-related information (on testing, the curriculum, learning problems, and more) along with other vital information you need to know about being a parent.

THE STUDY SKILLS HANDBOOK:
More than 75 Strategies for Better Learning
by Judith Dodge (Scholastic Trade, 1994)

A lively, oversize paperback with lots of strategies for frustrated parents and kids to help everyone focus on the work, rather than the battle.

PLAYGROUND POLITICS:
Understanding the Emotional Life of Your School-Age Child
by Stanley I. Greenspan (Addison-Wesley, 1993)

Greenspan, a psychiatrist and authority on child development, describes the stages of normal emotional development from ages five to twelve. Chapters One, Four, and Five, which explore the psychological foundations of learning and offer much sound advice on handling learning problems, are especially useful.

WHEN YOU WORRY ABOUT THE CHILD YOU LOVE:
Emotional and Learning Problems in Children
by Edward Hallowell (Simon & Schuster, 1996)

A new and enormously reassuring book by a Harvard Medical School professor and founder of the Hallowell Center for Cognitive and Emotional Health, who suffers from attention deficit disorder. Hallowell explains the biological basis for a wide range of childhood behavioral problems such as acting up in school and shows parents how to identify them and how to get the help you need.

KEEPING KIDS READING:
How to Raise Avid Readers in the Video Age
by Mary Leonhardt (Crown, 1996)

Packed with strategies and tips on how to instill a love of reading in your children from preschool through high school, this book by a veteran English teacher also offers fascinating observations on why kids read what they do. Her tips on dealing with children who have learning problems are excellent. Two chapters cover homework and common questions parents have about reading and school. Leonhardt is also the author of the easy-to-read, inspiring book, *Parents Who Love Reading, Kids Who Don't* (1993).

YOU CAN'T SAY YOU CAN'T PLAY
by Vivian Gussin Paley
(Harvard University Press, 1992)

This very simple book by a University of Chicago Lab School kindergarten teacher and MacArthur fellow offers a school-based solution to the issue most kids face at one point or another: feeling left out. Paley's account of her experiment with a "you can't say you can't play" rule also offers great insight into why kids are so excluding and how to help them with their feelings. An excellent book to share with teachers at your child's school.

THE HOMEWORK PLAN:
A PARENT'S GUIDE TO HELPING KIDS EXCEL
by Linda Sonna, Ph.D.
(Berkley Publishing Group, 1994)

This educational expert/psychologist offers several strategies to help kids stay motivated. Particularly focused for working parents who want to help kids learn to set up their own schedules.

SMART KIDS WITH SCHOOL PROBLEMS:
Things to Know & Ways to Help
by Priscilla L. Vail (Plume, 1989)

A great book for any parent who has said, "I don't get it! He's so smart. Why is he doing so poorly?" Vail, a lucid writer and highly experienced learning specialist, really covers it all. Includes specific remedial programs and testing techniques, as well as information on how to break the cycle of anger and low self-esteem. Also check out one of Vail's other books: *Gifted, Precocious, or Just Plain Smart* (1987).

SCHOLASTIC HOMEWORK REFERENCE SERIES:
EVERYTHING YOU NEED TO KNOW ABOUT MATH/SCIENCE/ENGLISH/AMERICAN HISTORY
by Anne Zeman and Kate Kelly
(Scholastic Trade, 1994)

This series of books, each one subject-specific, is designed to help parents of fourth, fifth, and sixth graders bone up on the basics so that they can help their kids with homework. They contain facts, formulas, photos, charts, maps, and timelines.

THE INTERNET

The Internet is an excellent source for information and support on many school-related issues. These sites are particularly helpful.

ADD—MYTHS AND FACTS

http://www.elite.net/%7Ebrownie/education/add_myths.html

This is a reassuring place for parents to go if they're worried about ADD or ADHD. It lists many myths and corrects them with useful information.

AGGGH! HOMEWORK

http://www.ezin.net/personal/artist/homewrk.htm

One of my favorite homework sites, it's primarily a source of fabulous enrichment on many subjects— science, geography, social studies, math, history, reference, on-line field trips, and more. Ideal for middle-school kids who want to dig a bit deeper.

THE BIG PAGE OF SPECIAL ED LINKS

http://www.mts.net/~jgreenco/special.html

A wonderful page for parents of kids with learning problems. Includes information about gifted and talented kids, ADD, books, catalogues, and a source for special toys for kids with learning disabilities.

JOHNS HOPKINS INSTITUTE FOR THE ACADEMIC ADVANCEMENT OF YOUTH

http://www.jhu.edu/~gifted/

This site will connect you to other sites for families of gifted kids, as well as inform you of the many special programs nationwide that are offered during the summer through the Center for Talented Youth.

LEARNING DISABILITIES ASSOCIATION (LDA)

http://www.ldanatl.org/Aindex.html

For parents who suspect or know that their child has a learning problem, this home page offers key resources, including: how to participate in the process of developing an Individual Educational Plan; a glossary of terms; an overview of legal issues; recent publications; and a fabulous bookstore that carries every related book in print for parents, kids, and teachers.

THE NATIONAL ASSOCIATION FOR GIFTED CHILDREN (NAGC)

e-mail: nagc@rmplc.co.uk

This Washington, D.C.-based organization is a terrific resource for parents of gifted kids, offering parenting advice, a list of publications and materials, and information on dealing with schools.

CD-ROM

There are literally hundreds of CD-ROMs available for kids that reinforce specific skills (math, writing, logic) as well as problem-solving skills. *Math Workshop,* mentioned on page 56, is a particularly good one. One fine source for all of these is the Educorp Direct catalogue, which offers titles, along with useful descriptions (phone: 1-800-843-9497). ❑